# 40 DAYS

## IN GOD'S PRESENCE

# 40 DAYS

## IN GOD'S PRESENCE

*A Devotional Encounter*

REBECCA BARLOW JORDAN

New York   Boston   Nashville

Unless otherwise noted, Scriptures are taken from the HOLY BIBLE, NEW IN-
TERNATIONAL VERSION®, NIV®. Copyright © 1973, 1978, 1984 by International Bible Society. Used by permission of Zondervan. All rights reserved.

Scriptures noted MSG are taken from THE MESSAGE. Copyright © Eugene H.
Peterson 1993, 1994, 1995. Used by permission of NavPress Publishing Group.

Scriptures noted KJV are taken from the King James Version of the Bible.

Scriptures noted NKJV are taken from the New King James Version. Copyright
© 1979, 1980, 1982 by Thomas Nelson, Inc. Used by permission. All rights reserved.

Scriptures noted TLB are taken from *The Living Bible*, copyright © 1971. Used by
permission of Tyndale House Publishers, Inc., Wheaton, Illinois 60189. All rights
reserved.

Warner Faith
Time Warner Book Group
1271 Avenue of the Americas, New York, NY 10020
Visit our Web site at www.warnerfaith.com.

Warner Faith® and the Warner Faith logo are trademarks of Time Warner Book
Group, Inc.

Printed in the United States of America
First Edition: January 2006
10 9 8 7 6 5 4 3 2 1

Library of Congress Cataloging-in-Publication Data
Jordan, Rebecca.
    40 days in God's presence : a devotional encounter / Rebecca Barlow Jordan.
        p.   cm.
    "Warner faith".
    Includes bibliographical references.
    ISBN 0-446-57786-3
    1. Bible—Devotional literature. I. Title: Forty days in God's presence. II. Title.
    BS491.5.J67 2006
    242'.2—dc22                                                    2005017444

To every person who has ever

yearned to know and enjoy more

of God's presence

# CONTENTS

# SPECIAL THANKS

No one ever works alone in birthing a dream. I could never thank those enough who have played such a vital role in the birth and development of this book.

Thanks to my friend and agent, Steve Laube, who understood the writing passion of my heart and who helped to develop an initial idea into a reachable dream. Thank you for believing in me as an author and for finding such a wonderful home for my heart's work.

Thanks to Leslie Peterson, my editor at Warner Faith, for literally "standing up" for my manuscript because you believed in its message from the beginning. Thank you for making a place to help nurture and grow this dream, and for shaping it into its final reality. Thanks to Rolf Zettersten, publisher of Warner Faith, who was willing to listen and believe and work to help place this manuscript. Thank you for making this book possible. Thanks to Leslie's assistant, Jennette Merwin, for ushering this book further through the process and for taking care of all the necessary details to bring about a finished product. To all the staff, sales and marketing teams, and all those who have worked behind the scenes at Warner Faith and Time Warner Book Group to help birth this book, I appreciate all of you so much.

Thanks to my family members and friends, church members, Bible study class, and my faithful prayer support team of women—Mary, Priscilla, Kim, Ruth, and Sharon—for all your prayers and encouragement. I felt your prayers, and this book would not be a reality without them.

Thanks to fellow authors, speakers, and friends who have inspired me with your words and prayers and encouragement, and who share the joy when a dream is born and a work is completed. Thanks to those who added their kind words of endorsement to this book.

A special thanks to my husband, Larry, whose encouragement, support, and example inspire me to keep writing. For all the mornings you gently reminded me with hot coffee and prayers to keep on track, for your crucial editing skills, for your passionate love and unselfishness that create in me a security and freedom to constantly seek and enjoy God's heart—how can I possibly say thank you enough? I love you!

And as always, more than anyone, thanks to the one whose love and faithfulness fills me with joy and purpose, and who daily draws me into his presence. For all the times I cried, "I can't do this," and he replied, "But I can," I am so grateful. Thanks to my constant companion, the Lord Jesus Christ, who forgives my faults, loves me unconditionally, and who gives me the wonderful privilege of writing about the Father's heart. He is the true dream-giver and the one who brings them to fulfillment.

Several years ago I asked a group of people the following question: "Do you enjoy God?"

The responses varied—from blank stares to "Not really," "I don't think so," "Well, maybe," "I'm not sure," and "No." So we spent some time talking about that very subject. While a few admitted that time and busyness prevented them from really enjoying God more, others hinted at deeper issues. All of them indicated they wanted to know God's presence in a deeper way.

May I get really personal? May I ask you the same question? Do you enjoy God? Do you long to experience his presence? If not, why? I can only guess your reasons. Perhaps it's because he has disappointed you. Your losses exceed your gains, and you don't understand how a loving God could let that happen. Maybe it's because you see no need for God. Your life has more gains than losses. Why do you need a crutch like some other people?

Maybe you don't really understand how to enjoy God's presence. He's too . . . demanding. Too heavenly. Too distant. Too harsh. Too unconcerned. Too busy. Maybe you're afraid of his presence. Or maybe someone told you it's not really possible to enjoy God personally. Or worse still, that you're not even *supposed* to. Or maybe it's because you don't know him— don't *know* him intimately.

If you can identify with any of these feelings, would you consider reading this book with an open mind and a listening heart? Climb into this "ark" of safety for a while and just watch and listen. Be skeptical if you wish, but at least be open.

And if you're already well acquainted with God and do know how to enjoy his presence, please also join me. In my four decades of walking with God, I keep finding new ways and reasons to enjoy him—and I fall in love with him again and again and again.

For all of you, my heart's desire is that as you sift through the pages of this book, you will begin to hear not only the gentle shower but also the mighty downpour of heaven's love, as you spend some quality time with God alone.

No doubt Noah really got to know his family well as they listened to the rain from heaven pelting their ark night after night. How did Noah feel, knowing that God had handpicked his family personally out of all the earth's population to continue the race? I wonder how his view of God enlarged even more? Did he truly understand the magnitude of what God was doing? And did he think about God's feelings for him? Did he ever wonder what would happen—if God didn't come through? Have you?

Can you imagine a God who would go to the lengths he did to preserve the human race standing ready to greet Noah when the doors of the ark were finally open and then changing his mind? Instead of a rainbow in the clouds, can you visualize God clicking his tongue at Noah and saying, "Sorry, Noah, I was only kidding. Bye!" Can you see him zap the survivors with a leftover lightning bolt and destroy the remnant of the world he had so carefully preserved? I don't think so. God has never been unfaithful. And although we can't read Noah's thoughts, we can assume the same faith that helped him build the ark not only sustained him, but grew even deeper throughout the entire storm (see Heb. 11:7).

During these forty days and nights, I pray you will come to know and experience God's presence—really know him as never before. I pray that when you're finished and the flood has subsided, like Noah you will not be the same person. I pray that a rainbow of joy will greet you as you step out of these pages and continue your joyful journey with the one who waits for your fellowship daily.

Richard Foster says, "The love of the Father is like a sudden rain shower that will pour forth when you least expect it, catching you up into wonder and praise and unspeakable speech. When this happens, do not put up an umbrella to protect yourself but rather stand in the drenching rain of the Father."[1]

I challenge you to spend forty days in his presence. Observe his ways. Study his heart. Learn who he is and how he longs to fellowship with you. And each time God sends a shower, may his heavenly "rain" soak you thoroughly. God preserved people because he loves them, because he cares for them, and because he wants to enjoy their presence daily. I believe he wants us to enjoy his presence, too.

I pray this book will help you do just that.

Rebecca

# 40 DAYS

## IN GOD'S PRESENCE

# THE GOD WHO WHISPERS

*After the wind there was an earthquake, but the LORD*
  *was not in the earthquake.*
*After the earthquake came a fire, but the LORD was*
  *not in the fire.*
*And after the fire came a gentle whisper.*

—1 Kings 19:11–12

The mighty prophet Elijah had witnessed a powerful, miraculous event: a standoff between good and evil. In true Lord of the Rings style, God had destroyed the altar of Baal, a false god, along with a host of Baal's followers. God had answered Elijah's prayer: "that these people will know that you, O LORD, are God, and that you are turning their hearts back again" (1 Kings 18:37).

The drama continued, however, when wicked Queen Jezebel cried revenge. Elijah, mighty man of God, suddenly turned into the coward of Judah County and ran for the hills. Depressed and suicidal, he begged God to take his life.

Exhaustion and stress affect even great leaders. After all, Elijah had just *run* about a hundred miles to escape death by the angry Queen Jezebel (1 Kings 19:1–3). But God had not abandoned his purpose for Elijah or his people. Between bouts of the prophet's exhaustion and sleep, the angel of God provided food and water that ultimately fueled Elijah for a forty-day-and-night journey to Mount Horeb, the mountain of God.

Elijah felt totally alone, abandoned, and afraid. There, he heard from God and pleaded his martyr case before the Lord: "I've been working my heart out for . . . God . . . [because] the people of Israel have abandoned your covenant, destroyed the places of worship, and murdered your prophets. I'm the only one left, and now they're trying to kill me" (1 Kings 19:10 MSG).

> There are times in our lives when God knows only a personal encounter will do. Elijah had walked with God and knew him personally.

There are times in our lives when God knows only a personal encounter will do. Elijah had walked with God and knew him personally. God's mantle of power and his hand of protection had sustained Elijah through many dangers. Now, just like a horse who had been knocked down, brutally wounded while protecting the one he loved, Elijah's spirit lay bared and bleeding.

But God does not shoot his wounded. The Bible says "a bruised reed he will not break, / and a smoldering wick he will not snuff out" (Isa. 42:3). Instead, God prepared Elijah for yet another divine moment—one with his name on it: "Go out and stand on the mountain in the presence of the LORD, for the LORD is about to pass by" (1 Kings 19:11). It was time for the Expert to do his supernatural work.

I'm sure Elijah prepared himself for disaster when a tornadic wind suddenly blew across the mountain, hurling and shattering rocks all around him. But God did not speak then. An earthquake split the ground, followed by a raging fire. With each act of nature, perhaps Elijah braced himself to be swallowed up, blown away, or consumed by the hands of this powerful God.

Yet God remained silent. Forever-like moments passed, then very clearly the voice of God spoke. That Elijah heard it at all is a wonder, after just witnessing scenes out of a miniature Armageddon. But the one whose spirit longs for restoration will not miss the gentle whisper of God as he speaks to the very soul—no matter how long it takes. Elijah moved close to the edge of the cave so he would hear every word.

What followed next was not an astounding truth, just the same question God had asked Elijah only moments previously. It was a question like the one God spoke to Adam: "Where are you?" when he knew exactly where to find Adam. Or like Jesus' question to Peter: "Do you love me?" when he knew full well the answer.

God simply whispered to the prophet, "What are you doing here, Elijah?" (1 Kings 19:13). Poor Elijah. Still shaking with deep-rooted fear, he blurted the same answer again. But God knew the inmost secrets of Elijah's heart. Gently, patiently, he breathed hope into his "wounded horse." He encouraged Elijah with specific instructions exactly at his point of need, to let him know he was not a lone ranger and not a condemned, useless survivor. He said, "Anoint two good kings who will finish destroying the Baal worshipers. Anoint your new future prophet successor (Elisha). And P.S.: You are not alone. Seven thousand others like you have not bowed the knee to Baal" (See 1 Kings 19:15-18).

> The one whose spirit longs for restoration will not miss the gentle whisper of God as he speaks to the very soul—no matter how long it takes.

The God Who Whispers revived Elijah's spirit for many

more years of service and productivity. Years later, Elijah's life ended, not in a glue factory, but in a blaze of glory.

We long for great encounters in our lives, for noble adventures, and for clear direction. But when the fight is gone and the divine voice is silent, it's easy then to feel the abandonment of a holy and personal God, the absence of divine fellowship.

But if we listen carefully following the thunderous noise of our calamities, while we are still licking our wounds we will hear it too. Like Elijah, we will hear the unmistakable, audible whisper of God, gently and patiently letting us know he is in control, he has the resources for battle, we are not alone, and God is not finished with us yet.

Who wouldn't enjoy that kind of God, who loves us so personally?

### PERSONAL TRUTH

*Whether God whispers or shouts in our pain is up to him. Our job is simply to keep listening.*

### PERSONAL PRAYER

*Lord, still the beating of my heart and the bleeding of my wounds long enough for me to hear your voice. When you whisper, may I always receive it as "sweet somethings" in my ear.*

### PERSONAL QUESTION

*What has God been whispering to you lately?*

# THE GOD OF KITCHEN DUTY

*All who were sitting in the Sanhedrin looked intently at Stephen,*
*and they saw that his face was like the face of an angel.*

—Acts 6:15

Many would have chafed under the assignment of "kitchen duty." Their ideas and aspirations of doing great things for God would definitely not include waiting tables or distributing food to some complaining, jealous women. Can you hear their protests? "I was made for better things!" "What am I doing in this hot, smelly kitchen?"

But not Stephen. Acts describes Stephen as a man "full of God's grace and power" (Acts 6:8). The new church in Antioch had chosen some men who had the touch of God on their lives to minister to the widows of their church. Their appointed duties would free the apostles to accomplish their work of preaching and teaching of the Word. Stephen was one of those men assigned to "kitchen duty."

Oswald Chambers says:

*Drudgery is one of the finest tests to determine the genuineness of our character. Drudgery is work that is far removed from anything we think of as ideal work. It is the utterly hard, menial, tiresome, and dirty work. And when we experience it, our spirituality is instantly tested and we will know whether or not we are spiritually genuine. . . . The inspiration of God is required if drudgery is to shine with the light of God upon it. In some cases the way a person does a task makes that work sanctified and holy forever. . . . When the Lord does something through us, He always transforms it.*[2]

**Many would have chafed under the assignment of "kitchen duty."**

The sixteenth-century Brother Lawrence, who called himself "the lord of all pots and pans," initially fought against his kitchen duty, but God soon changed his heart. He realized the power of submitting to God's Spirit: "The time of business," said he, "does not with me differ from the time of prayer, and in the noise and clutter of my kitchen, while several persons are at the same time calling for different things, I possess God in as great tranquility as if I were upon my knees at the blessed sacrament."[3]

Stephen must have possessed the same powerful secret. Soon after he accepted his assignment, Scripture records Stephen doing "great wonders and miraculous signs among the people" (Acts 6:8). Stephen's words and great wonders angered his enemies, and they began arguing with him. But just as in similar conversations with Jesus himself, these Jewish leaders could not refute Stephen's wisdom or "the spirit by whom he spoke" (Acts 6:10). The joy of Jesus shone through. A holy glow appeared around the face of Stephen, giving him the appearance of an angel that even his enemies noticed.

Incensed further, they trumped up blasphemy charges. Only after listening to Stephen expound the entire gospel message in a nutshell, from Abraham to Jesus, did Stephen's enemies explode with the same fury as some did when crucifying Jesus.

But God looked down on his servant Stephen, who was still full of the Spirit, and allowed him a glimpse of his glory. Not only that, the Bible records Jesus not *sitting* at the right hand of God—as do most passages of Scripture since Jesus' resurrection—but Jesus *standing* as if to applaud and honor Stephen's faithfulness (Acts 7:55).

Many of God's children have exclaimed from their deathbeds of suffering, only moments before their passing, their delight in seeing a great light, angels, loved ones waiting to see them—and even Jesus himself. But in Stephen's case, Jesus was standing to welcome Stephen home. And Stephen was so caught up in the moment, he described exactly what he was seeing to all who could hear.

This further fueled the Jewish leaders' anger and accusations of blasphemy. They had listened to Stephen quote Scripture, pointing out their refusal to believe Jesus and proving their guilt in Jesus' death. Not wanting to accept any blame in Jesus' crucifixion, the Jewish leaders had Stephen stoned.

Stephen's words—and his face—revealed the secret of his holy boldness: when God's Spirit consumes us, we are like actors playing out our divinely assigned part in heaven's dramatic history. Stephen enjoyed God immensely and knew God powerfully. I wonder how much of that joy and power grew out of his willing "kitchen duty."

> When God captures our hearts and we understand his greater purpose in our lives, the most ordinary drudgery will not repel us.

God's Holy Spirit continued the work he had already begun in Stephen: from dishpan hands to the face of an angel. And with Stephen's death, the world suddenly mourned the loss of the first Christian martyr.

When God captures our hearts and we understand his

greater purpose in our lives, the most ordinary drudgery will not repel us. It will actually enhance our enjoyment of this powerful God of Kitchen Duty.

### Personal Truth

*Powerful works and personal joy begin with submissive hearts.*

### Personal Prayer

*Holy Spirit, fill me with an unquenchable desire to turn ordinary moments into extraordinary lessons. Lord, I surrender to the work you have called me to do—whether in a palace or a kitchen.*

### Personal Question

*What "kitchen duty" has God called you to do?*

# THE GOD WHO IS
# SLOW TO ANGER

*Whenever the rainbow appears in the clouds, I will see it*
*and remember the everlasting covenant between God*
*and all living creatures of every kind on the earth.*

—Genesis 9:16

Does God get angry?

When Adam and Eve sinned, God had to remove them from their beautiful paradise garden. Still, in a flooding emotion of love and compassion, God planted a seed of hope as he promised a way of restoration in his words to the serpent:

> *I will put enmity*
> *    between you and the woman,*
> *and between your offspring and hers;*
> *    he will crush your head,*
> *and you will strike his heel.* (Genesis 3:15)

Later, at a period of history when the earth was greatly populated, God saw how the progression of evil had reached an all-time high. It was the worst of times, and it was the worst of times. The Bible says this about God's feelings: "The Lord was grieved that he had made man on the earth, and his heart was filled with pain" (Gen. 6:6).

God is a holy God, perfect, and he cannot accept sinful behavior. *Grieved* here carries the meaning of sighing, or breathing strongly as if angered or hurt deeply. By nature, God must act in order to console his own perfect character against such widespread rebellion. His purposes for discipline are always to bring repentance and a restoration of fellowship. But when his creation rejects that, and when man has trampled God's holy purpose, God must then bring judgment.

> God's purposes for discipline are always to bring repentance and a restoration of fellowship.

Most who understand the grief process know that grief and anger go hand in hand; before healing can come, anger must be dealt with. In a sense, perhaps that's what we see happening with the Flood. God was pained to the core. Like a knife going through his heart, his emotions were both anger at man for turning his back on God and sorrow that he had to "cut his losses" and start over.

So how did God handle those feelings? What could he do? Wipe everyone off the face of the earth? That was his first thought. And then he remembered Noah—"a righteous man, blameless among the people of his time, and he walked with God" (Gen. 6:9). Noah, the lone soul that stole God's heart, the only human living on earth at that time who chose to follow God—against the backdrop of an entire world that wouldn't. Noah was the only man who knew how to enjoy God.

But because God is truly "slow to anger, abounding in love"

(Num. 14:18), he chose to salvage a remnant of his creation. He planned to start over, with Noah. This man who loved God and who had never seen rain worked tirelessly for decades to build a self-contained houseboat longer than a football field. Then, for forty days and forty nights God sent a hurricane from heaven to flood the earth. And everything and everyone died that was not shut up in the ark that God and Noah built. God's anger was avenged.

Almost a year later Noah, his family, and the rest of the paired creations that God spared walked or flew out of the ark to dry ground. The first thing Noah did was give public thanks to God through a sacrificial burnt offering. God must have uttered the words in his heart, "It is good"; the Bible says Noah's gift pleased God (Gen. 8:21).

So God made some promises to Noah: As long as earth existed, Noah could count on the seasons, on day and night—on a restoration of the original order that God created. And God would never again destroy all living creatures by flood, even if sin completely consumed man's heart again.

The one evidence of God's promise we all remember is his gift of the rainbow. For as long as I can recall, I have viewed this multi-colored wonder as God's personal promise to *me*—to *us*—that a flood will not destroy our world. And that's true. But I believe there's more. God said whenever he sent the clouds, rain, and accompanying rainbow, it would be a sign, a covenant, a reminder to *him*. That

> That rainbow of hope would remind him and us that the flood of his anger had abated.

rainbow of hope would remind him and us that the flood of his anger had abated. Could a divine God ever forget a promise? No, but even Moses reminded God of his promises years later when God's anger waxed hot against his rebellious people (See Exod. 32:9-13).

The rainbow was a reminder to God to continue extending mercy to mankind as long as anyone walked the earth—a promise never again to deal with man in the same way. Perhaps it also reminded God that he made man for his pleasure and for man to enjoy him. How many times through the pages of history have man's actions and attitudes tested God's patience? And how many times has he looked at that rainbow, remembered his covenant to us, and relinquished his anger?

God's rainbow covenant was a continuation of a plan already formulated and one, thousands of years later, to be fully consummated. When God poured out all his holy anger, his grief and pain, on his own Son, making him the sweet sacrifice for man's rebellion, God was saying to the world for all time, "See? Here is my final proof that I am indeed a God of love and compassion, and that I want true joy for you. I really am a God who is slow to anger. I did not give you what you deserved. I did not send my Son to condemn the world or to destroy it with the flood of my righteous anger, but to save the world I love through him. Now, you can never question my intentions again."

And along with Noah, all the people said, "It is good."

## PERSONAL TRUTH

*When it rains, it pours. But when he reigns, the Son shines.*

## PERSONAL PRAYER

*Lord, when I was sinking in the waters of my own rebellion, you drew me out and placed me on solid ground. And when I should have received the flood of your holy anger, you wrapped your lov-*

*ing arms around me and called me your child. As long as I have breath, I will give you thanks.*

## PERSONAL QUESTION

*What does God's rainbow promise mean to you personally?*

# God the Mysterious Pursuer

*Surely the LORD is in this place, and I was not aware of it.*

—Genesis 28:16

Two brothers, completely different, were born to Isaac and Rebecca. One was a "wild man," a hunter, a man of the open country. He was the kind who probably bragged on how much game he'd bagged in one season, a man who could have lined his tents with trophy bucks and rich furs from his kills. The firstborn, his father Isaac's favorite—this was Esau.

Grasping for his father's blessing since birth, the second-born entered the world with one hand holding firmly to his brother's heel. Gentle, sensitive, and quiet, this twin named Jacob was anything but identical in personality and temperament. He preferred cooking wild game in the kitchen, hanging around the tents with his mom. Guess who Rebecca favored?

Jacob's name meant "he grasps the heel" or "he deceives." *Esau*, on the other hand, meant "hairy," but he was also called *Edom*, which meant "red." Each man lived up to his name.

One day after an exhausting hunting trip, Esau returned

home, starving for the red stew his brother was cooking. Tricky Jacob made a deal: "Make me a trade: my stew for your rights as the firstborn" (Gen. 25:31 MSG).

Esau's stomach growled like a lion stalking his prey. His hunger pains were so great he thought he was going to die. What good was a birthright to him if he was dead? So what did Esau do? "Edom-up!"

> God will go to any length, breadth, height, or depth to pursue the recipient of his blessing.

After Jacob "stole" the family birthright from Esau, he found himself running for his life at the prodding of his own mother. Anxiety, fear, and uncertainty must have accompanied Jacob on his flight from certain death at the hands of his angry brother. But what Jacob did not know was that God would pursue—and catch up to—him before Esau even located him.

It took a dream for God to get Jacob's attention—a ladder extended from heaven to earth, with God's angels descending and ascending on it. At the top of the ladder stood God himself, reminding Jacob he was the "God of your father Abraham and the God of Isaac." In that dream, God revealed himself to Jacob, reaffirming his covenant and his future plans for Jacob with a promise as solid as the rock on which he was sleeping: "All peoples on earth will be blessed through you and your offspring. I am with you and will watch over you wherever you go, and I will bring you back to this land. I will not leave you until I have done what I have promised you" (Gen. 28:13–15).

God wanted Jacob to know him. He pursued him to assure Jacob of his trustworthy character. It would not be the last time Jacob encountered the true, living God.

God will go to any length, breadth, height, or depth to pursue the recipient of his blessing. The covenant he first made with Abraham would continue through Abe's grandchildren, great-grandchildren, and their descendants. Although Jacob faced fear again, God worked patiently to complete his plans for this man.

When Jacob awoke from his dream, how did he know he had encountered a supernatural God? Was it the lingering aroma of heaven that filled his nostrils? Or perhaps the acrid smell of smoke from God's fiery hand? Maybe the gentle rustling of angel wings? Or the sudden entrance of a deep-seated, unexplainable peace? Only Jacob could answer, but his words, "Surely the LORD is in this place," tell us one thing is certain: he was now aware of the divine presence of God.

Each time God pursues us and we encounter his presence, he allows us to know something more of himself to sustain us and empower us for our journey. He reveals something more of his desire to know us and enjoy our fellowship. His purpose is not to alarm us, threaten us, shame us, or discourage us. In Jacob's case, the telltale evidence was a reverent, awesome fear in his heart for God, the Mysterious Pursuer, who had visited him. He felt a presence greater than his senses could comprehend at the moment.

> Each time God pursues us, we learn to appreciate and enjoy a new facet of his character even more.

Each time God pursues us, we learn to appreciate and enjoy a new facet of his character even more. And though God's encounters are always unique to each person, depending upon his purpose and how much he wants to reveal at the moment, we can be assured of two things: (1) God always takes the initiative in pursuing, and (2) true, life-changing experiences with God always produce a reverent awe and awareness: "God was here!"

There is no mistake. When God shows up, we will know it.

## Personal Truth

*God wants every person to have a personal encounter with him.*

## Personal Prayer

*Lord, sharpen my senses to hear your voice, see your face, smell your fragrance, and touch your heart when you come near. God, I want to enjoy and encounter you daily!*

## Personal Question

*When was the last time you had a true God encounter?*

# THE GOD OF RADICAL LOVE

*But love your enemies, do good to them,*
*and lend to them without expecting to get anything back.*

—Luke 6:35

In Jesus' famous Sermon on the Mount, he turned men's philosophies upside down. He was not turning out to be what the people had expected. Where was the king who would ride in on a white horse, setting the captive free from Roman rule, crushing the heads of their enemies underfoot? Where was the long-promised warrior who would destroy all evil and right all wrongs?

The multitudes had followed Jesus' miracles. They had seen or heard of his quieting a crazed man, restoring him to normalcy. The sick, the leprous, the lame, the demon-possessed—all experienced his divine touch. Jesus' teachings enthralled the people who listened. Many crept closer, drawn by curiosity to see this one whose fame had spread for miles. Who wouldn't enjoy this kind of God, who ordered numb limbs to walk, deaf ears to hear, and high fevers to break?

But there was more to this man Jesus, something his followers could not understand. His words did not match their expectations. Love their enemies? Love the hateful tyrants who had overtaxed, overburdened, and overstepped their boundaries of authority? Love those who had misused, hated, betrayed, and complicated their lives?

How could this possibly be the one they had set their hearts on for centuries? Things didn't compute. Their ideas didn't match up.

> Love is the one thing that can reduce a hardened heart to putty.

Jesus not only confused people's theology, his teaching required action and belief. This was no free ride. Loving one's enemies was such a radical thought only the true seeker and believer would receive it. But Jesus also offered free gifts: peace, joy, freedom, forgiveness, and yes, a radical kind of love. Only those who continued to follow Jesus—only those who would embrace his Father's heart—would understand in time the truth of Jesus' powerful words.

When we fall in love with Jesus, when he consumes the passions of our hearts, he replaces the old fires of vengeance and hatred. Jesus does not issue us rose-colored glasses but faith-filled hearts big enough to embrace a new kind of radical love. Love is the one thing that can reduce a hardened heart to putty.

Henry Drummond says, "Where Love is, God is. . . . God is love. Therefore *love*. Lavish it upon the poor, where it is very easy; especially upon the rich, who often need it most; most of all upon our equals, where it is very difficult, and for whom perhaps we each do least of all." He adds, "Souls are made sweet not by taking the acid fluids out, but by putting something in—a great Love, a new Spirit, the Spirit of Christ. Christ, the Spirit of Christ, interpenetrating ours, sweetens, purifies, transforms all. This only can eradicate what is wrong, work a chemical change, renovate and regenerate, and rehabilitate the inner man."[4]

When Jesus taught "Love your enemies," he mirrored that truth repeatedly, even until his last breath. Surrounded by enemies and friends alike, Jesus cried one of the strongest love prayers ever recorded. Those who heard him could not question the integrity of his heart and mission on earth, if they truly understood the magnitude of his words.

Can we truly *enjoy* a God of that proportion and persuasion? We can. Not only that, God tells us, when we flesh out that command and truly refuse to seek revenge on those who hurt us, by loving them and *blessing* them, we inherit a *blessing* ourselves: "Do not repay evil with evil or insult with insult, but with blessing because to this you were called so that you may inherit a blessing" (1 Pet. 3:9).

When from the deepest recesses of our hearts, we can cry out with Jesus in the face of our perpetrators, "Father, forgive them; they don't know what they're doing" (Luke 23:34 MSG), we can know something of the heart of Jesus. Is there a greater blessing than this?

Loving our enemies is valid proof of the passionate love Jesus placed in our hearts for him. Your enemies may not respect your love, or the spirit of joy in which you offer it; they may not receive it, and they probably won't understand it. You won't either. But when it happens, you'll know something about Jesus' passionate love for you—and you'll never be satisfied with anything less.

> Loving our enemies is valid proof of the passionate love Jesus placed in our hearts for him.

## PERSONAL TRUTH

*Jesus' love is the one force that can transcend every barrier ever known.*

## PERSONAL PRAYER

*Jesus, I know little of the kind of love you taught and mirrored, but I want to know. Stamp your love on my heart so deep that with every beat, it cries to everyone near, "I love you, I love you, I love you!"*

## PERSONAL QUESTION

*How can you show love to your "enemies" this week?*

# The God of Detours

*When Pharaoh let the people go, God did not lead them on
   the road
through the Philistine country, though that was shorter. . . .
God led the people around by the desert road toward the
   Red Sea.*

—Exodus 13:17–18

The Israelites had lived in oppression for four centuries. Their situation had grown progressively worse, until God intervened and raised up Israel's new deliverer and "prince of Egypt," Moses. They watched Pharaoh harden his heart repeatedly as one plague after another touched the Egyptians. The final plague that broke the brick-makers' bondage was the killing of the Egyptian's firstborn sons. According to God's instructions, the angel of death passed over every house where his people had sprinkled blood on the doorposts, saving their sons. The rest suffered the consequences.

When Pharaoh finally relented and freedom arrived, God wanted to show himself faithful and set the Israelite feet dancing through the dry Red Sea. But not immediately. First, he took them on a slight detour. God purposely did not lead them directly into battle. Why? They would have melted under the hot hands of their new enemies, the Philistines. Their wounds from slavery were too raw to be covered by useless armor.

God is a gracious God. He knows what we can bear. He does not usually lead us from the frying pan into the furnace—at least not until he has prepared us, tested our faith, and toughened us for the journey. The Israelites left Egypt "armed for battle," yet God knew their hearts. They were not yet strong enough. God knew that in the heat of battle they "might change their minds and return to Egypt" (Exod. 13:18). And once God has brought us freedom, he does not intend for us to walk back into bondage!

> He does not usually lead us from the frying pan into the furnace—at least not until he has prepared us, tested our faith, and toughened us for the journey.

Did God's plan work? Absolutely. He never left their side, traveling "ahead of them in a pillar of cloud to guide them on their way and by night in a pillar of fire to give them light" (Exod. 13:21). God even planned a slight retreat so Pharaoh would think they were drained, deluded, and doomed to wander around hopelessly (see Exod. 14:1-3).

When Pharaoh and the Egyptians finally began to pursue the Israelites, God stepped in again, assuring Moses and his people that he would fight for them (see Exod. 14:14). And he did. The walls of the Red Sea rolled back like a carpet, allowing all of God's people to walk to safety. The Egyptians, confused and stuck in the mud, finally recognized their hopelessness. The last words recorded before they turned and began gasping for breath were: "Let's get away from the Israelites! The Lord is fighting for them against Egypt"(Exod.21-25). The returning waters swept them away; the Israelites won victory, and God received the glory.

We may not understand the multiple testing God allows us to endure or why he checks our spirits with a "not yet" at times. We don't understand indirect, delayed routes to success. But God knows when our own armor will fail, and he wants to strip us, like David who faced the giant Goliath, of every foolish bit of human armor for our own protection. Those who can trust God's mysterious ways will not grumble when he leads them through barren deserts instead of lush green pastures on the way to freedom.

It is not always to discipline us, but to protect us, that God has us take the long road to victory. To do otherwise would shortcut God's purpose for our lives and his glory. This would bring not freedom, but slavery under our old enemies; it would result not in success, but in premature destruction. God took his people through a desert route and insurmountable odds to reveal his power—and he never left them alone in their journey.

The next time you start to question God's desert route, think again. Oswald Chambers says, "Living a life of faith means never knowing where you are being led. But it does mean loving and knowing the One who is leading."[5] The God of Detours, the one who is leading us, always has our best interest at heart and has planned a future for us filled not with destruction, but with hope, joy, and success.

> It is not always to discipline us, but to protect us, that God has us take the long road to victory.

Would you rather fight your battles armed with human strength, or take a detour through the desert, trusting God's intimate presence to insulate you and guide you all the way?

## Personal Truth

*Enjoying God's presence means trusting him completely.*

## Personal Prayer

*God, should I ever question your ways or your timing, place a seal on my lips immediately. I trust your wisdom and your protection and want to follow you wherever you lead me—even through the detours of life.*

## Personal Question

*When was the last time God took you on a detour that turned out in your best interests?*

DAY 7

# THE GOD OF VISUAL LESSONS

*Go down to the potter's house, and there I will give you*
*my message.*

—Jeremiah 18:2

I never hear God speak to me. How do you know he is speaking to you?"

The question is a familiar one. God's ways of speaking to us are as varied and as visual as they were in the Old Testament. He has not changed. We have. In the past, God spoke through prophets—special spokesmen for God such as Isaiah, Jeremiah, and Joel. Today, because of Jesus' death and resurrection, he speaks to us personally, especially through his Word. There, Jesus used many word pictures in his teaching and discipling on earth.

In one particular instance of God speaking to his prophets, he spoke a word of instruction to Jeremiah. The prophet did not hesitate; he simply obeyed. By then he was familiar with God's treasure hunts. And always, at the end of his journey, Jeremiah found the golden nugget of God's wonderful wisdom. So do all God's spokesmen.

God took Jeremiah to the home of a potter. Jeremiah stared steadily at the potter's wheel, mesmerized by the whirring and turning of the earthy lump on the wheel. Flecks of sticky clay

27

flew onto his hands and cloak as he observed the skill of the potter. At last, the pot looked finished. The potter held it up to examine it for flaws, only to discover it was seriously marred. Obviously ruined.

> God's ways of speaking to us are as varied and as visual as they were in the Old Testament.

So Jeremiah waited, anticipating the potter's next move. The prophet fully expected the craftsman to discard the pot on the dump heap, pick up a fresh batch of clay, and start over. But wait. Instead, with one powerful movement, the potter crushed the vessel into a gooey glob of clay. And then he began again, shaping, tearing, mending, adding, stretching, until he had formed a perfectly designed creation.

Jeremiah said nothing. The potter said nothing. But suddenly God opened Jeremiah's spiritual eyes. And from the scene in front of Jeremiah, God formed his own metaphor and delivered it to Jeremiah's heart: "Watch this potter. In the same way that this potter works his clay, I work on you, people of Israel" (Jer. 18:6 MSG).

God's message was a clear word for Israel: God was the Potter. He was in control of the wheel. And he could do what he wanted with the clay, his people. Would they trust him and remain pliable in his hands? Their obedience or disobedience would determine their future.

Does God speak to us in visual color daily? Maybe you walk through a garden. A beautiful butterfly is suspended in midair, hanging as if by a magical thread. And then you look closer and see that the magical thread is part of a silky, shiny web of the butterfly's dreaded enemy. The spider has done his evil work. It is the survival of the fittest, yet you empathize with the butterfly and gently reach out and free its fragile wings. The insect flutters, then pauses, as if with gratitude. To move back into the clutches of the spider's web would be both deadly and foolish.

"You were made to fly!" you shout in victory, as if you have just pardoned a hundred prisoners with one act of kindness. And you watch the grateful butterfly as it lights on the petals of a nearby flower and begins to enjoy the sweet fragrance of the garden again.

If you are listening, you will hear what God has just said to you: "You—yes, you, my child—*you* were made to fly." And suddenly your eyes are opened, and you see your life before you, the harmful habits that have long snared you, just like the web. And God reminds you that only he has the power to free you. He is the one in control. But your obedience will determine the outcome. Will you stay in the clutches of the web? Or will you fly with new purpose for the one who has granted you freedom?

The truth is God still speaks loudly to us in his lessons: through the pages of Scripture; yes, through the warning of a friend; through piled-up wreckage along the road; through a child's simple prayers; through an artist at work; or through a garden stroll. God very much longs to teach us, to love us, to know us, to enjoy us, to use us, to speak to us.

It may be a word of warning, as God gave to Jeremiah. He may confront you about your damaging habit, or he may challenge you with a new opportunity. He may speak words of comfort or assurance in a time of great loss or need. He may offer counsel for a confusing situation. Or he may make you smile as he paints for you his picture of his love.

> To know God— to really hear his heart and enjoy his fellowship—is what God wants for us.

To know God—to really hear his heart and enjoy his fellowship—is what God wants for us. The question is, are we listening? Are we watching? Are we waiting? Are we seeing?

Our obedience will determine the outcome.

## PERSONAL TRUTH

*Insanity is staying in ruts when you know perfectly well how to get out.*

## PERSONAL PRAYER

*Lord, open the eyes of my heart that I might see your visual lessons around me. Open my ears that I might hear the truths that will ultimately free me to become all you want me to be.*

## PERSONAL QUESTION

*What visual lessons has God shown you recently?*

# THE GOD WHO IS WITH US

*But while Joseph was there in the prison, the LORD was with him;*
*he showed him kindness and granted him favor in the eyes of the prison warden.*

—Genesis 39:20–21

From the pit to Potiphar's prison—it hardly seemed fair. Joseph had been betrayed by his brothers, thrown into a pit, and then sold into slavery in Egypt. Potiphar, one of Pharaoh's officials, liked Joseph and allowed him to live in his house. Whatever was going on in Joseph's character was not bitterness. Potiphar noticed his unusual, sterling behavior and attributed his success to God: "His master recognized that GOD was with him, saw that GOD was working for good in everything he did" (Gen. 39:3 MSG).

Then Joseph was betrayed again, this time by Potiphar's own wife. Accused falsely of rape, Joseph was thrown into another "pit"—this time a prison. Yet even in Joseph's dark residence, God had not abandoned his servant: "The LORD was with him." And because God was with Joseph, he gave him favor in the mind of the prison warden.

When God is with us, we are not the only ones affected. It would have been easy for Joseph to think, "If I can just wait out my time and be good enough to earn a pardon, I will eventually break out of this place and experience freedom once again." But freedom had already found a place in Joseph's heart in spite of his circumstances. Well seasoned by hard times and God's grace, Joseph did not retaliate; neither did he strive on his own to persuade his keepers that he was innocent.

> When God is with us, we are not the only ones affected.

We are mistaken if we think we can turn the hearts of other people to deliver us from our plights of suffering. What we really need is the God Who Is with Us. When God's presence and God's blessing rest on us—by his choice, mercy, and grace—he is the one accomplishing the work and granting favor. He is the one who removes crusty scales of unbelief from our enemies' eyes. He is the one who places a holy glow of protection around our entire situation, if he so chooses. He is the one who gives dream interpretations, as he did for Joseph when two other prisoners, a cupbearer and the king's baker, needed explanations for their dreams: "Then Joseph said to them, 'Do not interpretations belong to God? Tell me your dreams' " (Gen. 40:8).

Then when Pharaoh himself had some troubling dreams, those two prisoners, now restored to their former positions, remembered Joseph's ability and told Pharaoh. Pharaoh was so impressed with the God of Joseph that he freed Joseph and put him in charge of the land of Egypt (Genesis 41:1-41).

Joseph nurtured his relationship with the God Who Is with Us. And he learned to enjoy and trust this amazing God. Pride could have turned the situation into a further disaster and put distance between Joseph, his God, and the ones around him. But Joseph took no credit for his divine, dream-revealing ability, and he took no revenge for his obvious injustice. And God continued to give him favor, directing Joseph and blessing him throughout his life.

I remember a time when I wondered who was in control. On summer vacations when I was a small girl, the five of us would pile into our sedan and head for the mountains, the beach, or some other interesting destination. Invariably, we traveled roads with hills—huge ones in the eyes of a six-year-old. Each time the road swung upward, I held my breath, eyes wide with fear. I just knew that once we reached the top of those high hills, we would plunge headlong into space and ultimately crash. And then our vacation would be spoiled.

But experience soon taught me that I really had no reason to live in a prison of fear. I'm sure during those times my father must have looked in the rearview mirror at my puffy, red face and wrinkled brow and just smiled. I soon learned a simple truth: Daddy was a good driver. And as long as my father was with us, driving the car, I had no reason to worry. He—not my fear—was in control. I could relax and enjoy the trip, wherever it took us. I learned to trust, because I knew Daddy would always bring us safely to our destination.

When our heavenly Father is with us, he is in charge; we are not. And in God's eyes, regardless of how circumstances appear at the moment, the results are always favorable in the end. No matter how difficult at the time, he will always bring us safely to the destination he has planned for us.

> When our heavenly Father is with us, he is in charge; we are not.

## PERSONAL TRUTH

*Only God can turn prisons into palaces.*

## PERSONAL PRAYER

*Lord, I may not see your hand at work with human eyes; I may not hear your voice with human ears. But your Spirit bears witness with my spirit that I indeed belong to you. It is not up to me to persuade, only to persist in trusting that you, the God Who Is with Us, is working out my past, present, and future.*

## PERSONAL QUESTION

*Are you dealing with any situations in which you need to remember that God is with you?*

# THE SOVEREIGN GOD

*Elisha died and was buried.*

—2 Kings 13:20

It's not easy trying to live up to the reputation of someone else's greatness.

In many ways, Elisha, like Joshua, was a "shadow leader." Each followed in the shadow of great men. Joshua succeeded Moses, while the younger prophet Elisha continued Elijah's legacy.

Both Joshua and Elisha's names meant "God is my salvation." Joshua accompanied Moses partway up Mount Sinai, where he waited in the shadow of the rocks while God wrote his commandments on stone with his own fingers. For years, this young aide observed Moses and saw Moses' miracles as well as his moods. God empowered Joshua to accomplish great things for him. It was Joshua who led the Israelite people to their long-awaited promised land across the Jordan River; Moses was forbidden to cross.

But try to imagine living up to this reputation: "For no one has ever shown the mighty power or performed the awesome deeds that Moses did in the sight of all Israel" (Deut. 34:21).

Elisha, too, faced a personal challenge in following greatness. Elisha's great feats and miracles were no less important

35

than Elijah's, and he performed twice as many miracles as his predecessor; but the older Elijah clearly seemed to have the advantage. At the end of his life, God honored the great prophet Elijah and welcomed him to heaven by beaming him up in a chariot dance in the middle of a whirlwind while his close disciple, Elisha, watched.

> God Almighty is just that: the almighty, sovereign God who plans, knows, and determines everything about our beginnings, endings, and the journeys in between.

Elisha's one request of Elijah: to receive a double portion of Elijah's spirit. He would receive the wish—if he caught a glimpse of Elijah's supernatural exodus into the heavens. Elisha watched the entire scenario and received Elijah's mantle along with the double portion of power.

Both achieved greatness. Yet their lives ended differently. Elisha grew ill. Why was one leader allowed to exit in a blaze of glory, while the other—the man who had preached God's words, miraculously healed others, and counseled kings—simply "died and was buried"? No fanfare, no miraculous intervention from God's almighty hand.

Centuries later Jesus, the Messiah—the salvation Elisha mirrored in Old Testament shadowy foretelling—was transfigured. Who appeared before the disciples' eyes along with Jesus? Not Joshua, not Elisha, but their strong mentors: Moses and Elijah (Mark 9:4). Elijah, once again privileged to participate in a dazzling display of God's power—the likes of which Elisha or Joshua had never seen. Why did God choose these two giants of the faith, and not them? It all could have seemed so unfair—if these two men had been into comparisons. But God knew what he was doing.

God Almighty is just that: the almighty, sovereign God who plans, knows, and determines everything about our beginnings, endings, and the journeys in between. It's one of the attributes most have difficulty understanding about God.

And we are left to wonder. Holding the mantle of a predecessor's reputation or influence, a coworker's achievements, or a sibling's personality, we may struggle to find our place. If we are into grand appearances and exits—if printing our names on the billboards of life replaces painting his name—we will never know or understand or enjoy God's true purpose for our lives.

Our tombstones, too, may read: "_____ died and was buried." But in God's great scheme of things, how we die is unimportant. It's not whether we leave in a blaze of glory, but whether we have blazed a trail of glory for our almighty God and for our successors—that really matters.

Elisha may have followed in the shadow of a great predecessor, but he soon emerged into the full light for which he was created. Elisha knew and enjoyed God personally, not because he was a superhero, but because he fulfilled his God-called purpose in life. Then he died.

What a wonderful legacy to leave for our successors!

## PERSONAL TRUTH

*A shadow is simply a mirrored image intercepting the greater Light's rays.*

## PERSONAL PRAYER

*God, I would rather serve you faithfully in the shadows and enjoy the sheer pleasure of your company than spend my days wondering why life isn't fair—and maybe miss your fellowship altogether.*

## PERSONAL QUESTION

*How do you handle walking in the shadows?*

# THE GOD OF ALL WISDOM AND KNOWLEDGE

*Ask for whatever you want me to give you.*

—2 Chronicles 1:7

Solomon was one of the wisest men of all times—or was he? Unfortunately, even those entrusted with great wisdom don't always act wisely.

After King David died, Solomon was the reigning king of Israel. He addressed the people at Moses' tent of meeting—the place in the desert where God made his presence known. David had moved the ark of God to Jerusalem, but the bronze altar still remained in Gibeon in front of the tabernacle. Solomon went to the altar and offered not one, but a thousand, burnt offerings on it.

Apparently God was pleased with the offerings, and later that night, Solomon had a divine encounter. God wanted to give Solomon the desires of his heart—a risky thing for God to offer any man. But our sovereign God already knew Solomon's heart. The king passed his first test of godly leadership by asking not for gold to fill his coffers, fame to build his name, success over his enemies, or death at a ripe old age; Solomon asked for wisdom and knowledge, "that I may lead this people, for who is able to govern this great people of yours?" (2 Chron. 1:10).

Underlying Solomon's words was a recognition of God's great wisdom and power—and of his own human inadequacy. Essentially, Solomon said, "I cannot lead your people as I am. I'm like a little child. I need you, God, and your wisdom. I need your heart and mind to take over mine."

> The God of All Wisdom and Knowledge loves to grant wisdom to those who ask.

That's the kind of prayer God cannot resist answering. Not only did Solomon receive his request, God gave him everything he could have asked for but didn't: honor and riches. Solomon became the wealthiest, wisest, and most famous king ever recorded. The Bible says God gave Solomon wisdom, insight, and understanding "as measureless as the sand on the seashore . . . greater than the wisdom of all the men of the East, and greater than the wisdom of Egypt. He was wiser than any other man" (1 Kings 4:29–31).

The God of All Wisdom and Knowledge loves to grant wisdom to those who ask (see James 1:5). When we seek to know God in such a way that will ultimately bless him and his people, God is pleased.

In the same way, God loves a cheerful giver—and Solomon planned to give his God-ordained wisdom away to lead God's people. After building a beautiful temple for the Lord, Solomon offered thousands of joyful sacrifices, filled with gratitude to the God he loved. His heart welled up with thanksgiving as he experienced God's awesome glory filling the completed temple.

Unfortunately, Solomon must have misplaced his wisdom along the way. He could probably identify with the story told by Bruce Larson of two women who saw each other at a party for the first time in many years: "After the initial delighted exchange of greetings, the first woman noticed that her friend was wearing an extraordinary diamond. She couldn't help commenting, 'That's the most beautiful and enormous diamond I've ever seen!'

" 'Yes, it's an unusual diamond,' was the reply. 'It's the Calahan Diamond. And it comes complete with the Calahan curse.'

" 'What's the Calahan curse?'

" 'Mr. Calahan!' she said."[6]

Along with Solomon's wealth came the curse of too many "Mrs. Solomons"—over a thousand wives and concubines. In the Bible, Solomon's book of Ecclesiastes offers the poignant warnings of a once-wise man who had "been there and done that." His disobedience to the Lord by marrying outside his faith created in Solomon a divided heart because of the women's loyalty to other gods (see 1 Kings 11:1–6). Because of God's promise to David, God delayed his discipline until after Solomon's death—when his kingdom, too, would be divided.

God loves a wise seeker. It almost seems as if we need wisdom in order to ask for wisdom—and then to maintain wisdom. Knowing and enjoying God personally requires insight and knowledge far beyond our human capacity. Perhaps when God recognizes a truly hungry heart, eager to know him and to give him honor, he gets so excited he just keeps pouring out every blessing he can think of.

> God loves a wise seeker.

But lest you start dreaming of padded bank accounts and your name in lights, remember that truly wise seekers want the Giver more than the added gifts he might send their way. And with those gifts comes the responsibility to handle all of them wisely. Wise seekers leave the answers, and the kind of blessings God chooses, up to the God of All Wisdom and Knowledge.

And wise seekers know how to enjoy and guard the wisdom God gives them.

### PERSONAL TRUTH

*A little wisdom aptly applied is better than gold hidden from sight.*

### PERSONAL PRAYER

*God, I need your wisdom in my life. Without it, every action, every decision, every thought is like a balloon without air. Breathe your Spirit into mine that I might know your heart and experience your wisdom and joy. You are my greatest treasure!*

### PERSONAL QUESTION

*In what areas do you most need God's wisdom?*

# THE GOD OF OUR DEFENSE

*Now Moses was a very humble man,*
*more humble than anyone else on the face of the earth.*

—Numbers 12:3

Have you ever known a big sister who didn't like to boss around her little brother when they were children? Occasionally the scenario could get out of hand. But what happens when the two grow up?

Miriam, Moses' big sister, found out. She started by picking on an in-law. A growing resentment led her to criticize Moses' Cushite wife, who was an Ethiopian, not a Jewish woman. Yet God had not given them laws against marrying foreigners until they moved later into the promised land. Miriam could have disliked his wife simply because she was not like them, but it's also possible Miriam used Moses' wife as an excuse to mask a deeper problem. At any rate, jealousy seemed to overshadow any awe or respect she might have had for Moses.

Perhaps in her mind, Miriam had never elevated Moses beyond "baby brother." And, after all, she *was* responsible for seeing that his life was saved as a baby. Didn't she make sure the beautiful Pharaoh's daughter saw him floating in the Nile? Who ran and got Mom so she could nurse Moses until it was time for him to go live at the palace? Who kept him from falling under Pharaoh's knife, as did all the other Hebrew babies of that time? Wasn't it because of her that Moses even lived to be used by God in such a great way? Moses should have been thanking her—and maybe acknowledging her keen spiritual insight.

> It is never wise to attack the character of God's anointed—even if that person happens to be your baby brother.

Miriam seized her opportunity, and her emotions soon escalated into something more serious. Even brother Aaron, Moses' spokesman, joined Miriam in her full-blown sibling rivalry and jealousy. When Miriam's bitterness finally spewed out, Aaron's voice chimed in too: "Has the LORD spoken only through Moses? Hasn't he also spoken through us?" (Num. 12:2).

Was this the same Miriam who, with tambourine in hand, had led the Israelite women in a dance of praise to God after crossing the Red Sea? What happened? We can only speculate that all this time Miriam's growing discontent was not about Moses, but about her relationship to God. Ultimately, it was all about pride.

Pride can manifest itself in many ways. It begins as a tiny nodule, a solitary thought or complaint, then grows and spreads like a cancer out of control. Pride puffs itself up with knowledge to cover its ignorance and deflates others who challenge its thinking. Pride lusts for its name in lights and the credit for a job well done. It doesn't question; it challenges—because it trusts no one else for the answers. Jealousy calls itself "concern," and even silence can mask a false humility and prideful spirit. This kind of pride cannot live in harmony with joy. And God will not tolerate it.

Overconfidence steals pride's so-called compassion and manages to hide its real insecurities only briefly. In time, the constant need to prove, to compare, or to think "unfair" rushes to the surface, only to tangle with the wrong person. Someone has aptly said, "As the chest swells, the brain and the heart shrink."[7] The Bible says that pride leads to destruction and ends in a fall (Prov. 16:18).

That's exactly what happened to Miriam. Somewhere through the years, as big sister saw little brother rise higher and higher, her resentment kicked in and Miriam's heart shrank. She lost the joy of being used years earlier to preserve a leader. Pride consumed her and she fell right into the hands of God.

God's response was not a happy one. It is never wise to attack the character of God's anointed—even if that person happens to be your baby brother. God's voice reminded Aaron and Miriam that Moses had a special relationship with him, one different from that of all other prophets. Hopefully, Miriam and Aaron heard God's *unspoken* insinuations as well: "and different from my relationship with both of you." God revealed himself to them through visions and dreams, but with Moses, God talked "face to face" (Num. 12:8).

Aaron immediately repented, but Miriam faced God's discipline for her rebellion—leprosy. Aaron pleaded for Moses to intervene. To his credit, Moses did not retaliate. Instead, his response proved his humility and solid relationship with God. He was a leader who had come to know, to trust, and to enjoy God. Moses asked God to heal Miriam from the leprosy.

> Moses didn't need to defend his own reputation. God did that for him.

God answered, and after seven days Miriam had a clean body—and no doubt, a clean heart again. We never hear another proud, rebellious word from her mouth. In fact, we hear nothing more of Miriam until her death.

The lessons here are multifaceted. Are God's leaders held more accountable than others? Undoubtedly so. But this God encounter also tells us something about God's relationship with his people. Moses didn't need to defend his own reputation. God did that for him.

But God's love was no less great for Miriam than it was for Moses. Centuries later, the prophet Micah warned God's people to repent—the same message God spoke through every prophet of his. But as he recounted God's activities and faithfulness through the years to his people, he also shared God's direct words. And God mentioned Miriam's name as a leader in the same sentence with her famous brother Moses: "I sent Moses to lead you, / also Aaron and Miriam" (Mic. 6:4). God's forgiveness is always complete, and he will restore his joy to anyone who wants to receive it.

It is always because of God's pure love that we are not consumed entirely. He is the God who defends—*and* the God who mends.

### PERSONAL TRUTH

*Criticism can steal our joy or deepen it.*

### PERSONAL PRAYER

*Lord, whatever good I can do will be only because you do it. More than anything, I want to see your name in lights, not mine; to speak your words, not mine; and to rejoice in the privilege of shar-*

*ing in your kingdom work. Forgive me for hidden or overt pride that tries to defend self, instead of letting you reveal the truth.*

## PERSONAL QUESTION

*How do you handle criticism?*

# THE GOD WHO KNOWS ALL

*O LORD, you have searched me*
*and you know me,*
*you know when I sit and when I rise;*
*you perceive my thoughts from afar.*
*. . . You are familiar with all my ways.*

—Psalm 139:1–3

What kind of God knows you so well that he can even read your thoughts from afar? What kind of God takes the time to know you so well that he searches you inside and out?

David was acquainted with such a God personally. This was no ordinary God—no carved image of wood or stone, no figment of some mystic's imagination. This was not some higher power that would intervene only in extreme crisis.

David felt "hemmed in, behind and before" by his God (Ps. 139:5), yet that made him a God of protection. This was the God who knew David, who even wrote the prescription for his birth and numbered every hair on David's head. This was a God whose thoughts about David outnumbered the grains of sand on every seashore, a God who ordained his purpose long before David uttered his first birth cry.

This faithful shepherd spent endless hours tending sheep

in the pastures, thinking about God, amazed at his awesome character. Throughout the Psalms, David spoke of God being our Fortress, our Refuge, our Strength, and our Salvation, the Lord Most High, the Mighty One. David, a shepherd himself, even referred fondly to the Lord as his own personal Shepherd. He walked through those valleys, rested in those green meadows, lived under the shadow of God's wings, and God kept him in the hollow of his hand.

> No one cracks the door of intimacy without desiring a personal relationship with another.

David's conclusions were always the same. This God, too powerful and otherworldly for David to understand, was nonetheless a personal God. David admitted "such knowledge is too wonderful for me, / too lofty to attain" (Ps. 139:6).

In his soliloquy to God, David couldn't resist sneaking in a human "if only" to God. "You are such an amazing God; *if only* you would deal with my enemies. After all, they are *your* enemies, too, Lord," David seemed to imply (see Ps. 139:19–22).

Yet David hastened to add at the end of Psalm 139 that his own thoughts about God would not remain only "head knowledge." His overall personal invitation to God opened the doors to the inner rooms of David's heart. No one cracks the door of intimacy without desiring a personal relationship with another. "You, who know my thoughts so well," he said, "God, search me. You who know my heart, come and really *know* my heart, and show me anything that is offensive to you. Lead me in 'the way everlasting'" (see Ps. 139:23–24). And God did that—many times.

As children we love to share secrets with our friends. Little girls, especially, run giggling to each other to unload the fun things they've just discovered. Teenagers choose confidantes more carefully. By the time we reach adulthood, trusting hearts begin to close up like spent flowers as skepticism floods our roots.

What makes us pull in our heads like turtles and retreat to a shell-like existence? Is it because one time we took a risk and shared a secret, only to find our best friend had blabbed it in the school lunchroom? Do we shrink in silence because we think it's wrong to express any negative feelings? Or do we clam up because we so desperately need the approval of others that we cannot risk their response? Our hearts long for someone we can trust completely, someone who will love us as we are, someone who knows before asking what's wrong and what to do about it. We want someone who will not laugh when we fall and skin our knees, one who will not abandon us when our failures are exposed, someone who understands our heart's deepest pain.

But Oswald Chambers says the sign of a real friend is not someone who unveils only troubles and sorrows. "Many people will confide their secret sorrows to you, but the final mark of intimacy is when they share their secret joys with you."[8] J. I. Packer says that as friends "open their hearts to each other by what they say and do, each 'tastes' the quality of the other, for sorrow or for joy. They have identified themselves with, and so are personally and emotionally involved in, each other's concerns. They feel for each other, as well as thinking of each other. This is an essential aspect of the knowledge which friends have of each other."[9]

Packer says it is the same way with our relationship with God. He adds, "Knowing God is more than knowing about him; it is a matter of dealing with him as he opens up to you, and being dealt with by him as he takes knowledge of you."[10] Why do we try to hide anything from God "since he knows the secrets of the heart?" (Psalm 44:21).

He is the God who knows and enjoys us so much that he is waiting for us to do the same: to know and enjoy his presence.

One man apparently didn't understand that God is truly a God Who Knows All. A father once allowed his son to accompany him on a mission to steal potatoes from a neighbor's farm. As they came to the fence, the father stopped and looked right and left for any observers. Seeing nothing and hearing nothing, he began to climb the fence and continue his plan. About that time the son spoke up: "Dad," he said, "you forgot something—you didn't look up."[11]

He is the God who created us, the God Who Knows All— good and bad. And He is a God who freely shares his secrets with us (Isa. 45:3 NIV, Psalm 25:14 NKJV). He is the God who knows and enjoys us so much that he is waiting for us to do the same: to know and enjoy his presence. David understood that. By inviting him into the rooms of our hearts with a divine searchlight, we, too, are responding in a personal way to a very personal God.

It is indeed the beginning of the "way everlasting."

## Personal Truth

*In an intimate relationship with the God Who Knows All, even painful discoveries turn to intense joy.*

## Personal Prayer

*God, you know me so well, but there is so much I still want to know about you. Thank you for thinking of me constantly. Search every part of my heart, and never stop teaching me. I will search for you with all my heart, soul, and mind, that I might really know and enjoy you intimately.*

## Personal Question

*Does God have access to all the rooms of your heart?*

# THE GOD WHO OPENS

# BLIND EYES

*One thing I know. I was blind but now I see!*

—John 9:25

I t was a common sight: the poor, the blind, the deaf, and
the lame, all gathered in places of prominence, in plain
view of the public. From early morning until dusk you could
hear their cries: "Have mercy on me!" "Alms for the poor!" At
the entrance of the city gates, on the outer court steps of the
synagogue, along the busy streets and market places—they
camped out, dependent on others for their livelihood.

There the homeless found a measure of respect, for good
pharisaical law keepers were expected to give alms to the
poor. Many leaders considered these offerings a source of
pride: they plunked their coins into the beggars' cups while
they themselves begged others to note their generosity.
Most Jews believed the inferior paupers suffered purely because of their sinfulness. Perhaps the Jewish Pharisees
viewed their offerings as grace gifts, tokens of pity to the
ones whose punishment for sin was the inability to see the
light as they did.

Jesus disciples' had also bought into the mistaken belief that sin caused all suffering. In an encounter with a blind beggar, their question was not, "Did this man sin?" but "Who sinned, this man or his parents, that he was born blind?" (John 9:2).

And Jesus surprised them all. "Neither this man nor his parents sinned, but this happened so that the work of God might be displayed in his life." Jesus continued by contrasting day and night. "As long as it is day, we must do the work of him who sent me. Night is coming, when no one can work. While I am in the world, I am the light of the world" (John 9:3–5).

> God is in the business of opening blind eyes.

The disciples must have wondered, was this another one of Jesus' riddles? What on earth did he mean? Jesus was giving them a preview not only of the miracle he was about to perform, but the purpose of his actions: God is in the business of opening blind eyes.

But Jesus was also reminding them there was a time limitation. When do we have full vision? During the daylight hours. When nighttime comes, sight is difficult. Like a blind man, we can neither see nor do the Father's work. And as long as God allows, until the end of the world, he and we are to join together in this all-important mission of helping others see. When God draws the curtain between now and eternity, this world, as we have known it, will disappear in darkness. A new world will emerge—one that God is preparing even now.

Jesus healed the blind beggar, and the man could see. Those who knew him heard the beggar's true confession and took him before the Pharisees, where he repeated his story of how he was healed. However, the Pharisees cared more about punishing lawbreakers than they did about granting mercy, so they deliberately tried to confuse the man and debate the authenticity of his story. But the man simply told the truth, bearing witness to what he knew: "One thing I know. I was blind but now I see!"

The Pharisees continued to question the man but were so enraged at his responses that they finally threw him out (John 9:34).

Then Jesus showed up again. The first time, he had opened the man's physical eyes and allowed the man to experience the healing power of God. The second time, he opened his spiritual eyes completely and revealed more: an understanding of his true identity.

To those who are prepared, Jesus is always willing to reveal himself and give deeper understanding. This former sightless seeker was so hungry, he believed immediately and worshiped Jesus for who he really was. The man was then free to fully display the work of God in his life. And he was then totally free to enjoy both his newfound sight and his newfound Savior.

In essence, Jesus said to the man he healed, "It is for blind men like you that I have come into the world—so you can see. Those who claim to see may actually be living in darkness" (see John 9:39).

Jesus answered the Pharisees' confusion of suffering and punishment again in his last response to the Pharisees' question: "What? Are we blind too?" (John 9:40). Jesus said if they were physically blind, sin would not be the cause. But to be spiritually blind and claim to have sight—that was a condition only sin caused. They were left to draw their own conclusions. Jesus already knew the answer.

I imagine some "enlightened" people once thought Robert

> To those who are prepared, Jesus is always willing to reveal himself and give deeper understanding.

Davis was blind, when he insisted his marriage would work during some dark times. A year after he and Estelle married, she lost her right arm in a factory accident when the limb ripped away from the socket. But Davis was a determined man: "Different people said we wouldn't make it. But my mind was made up when I asked her to marry me. I think we disappointed a whole lot of people by staying together."

If love is blind, then Robert Davis was blind. He bought his wife a car and equipped it with a special steering wheel, designed for ease by a one-armed person. He also worked two jobs, "whatever it took." Mrs. Davis adds, "He loved me through sickness, health and the five kids." (They lost one daughter early in their marriage.) She says their relationship was not love at first sight. Instead, Estelle admits, "we must have fallen in love somewhere along the way."

They freely admit they've had their share of dark days and problems like other couples. But they made it through. Fifty-one years later they are still walking in the light of a wonderful marriage and eagerly boast of their family that also now includes twelve grandchildren and seven great-grandchildren.[12] I wonder what those people who claimed to have light would say about Robert's "blindness" now—and about the marriage they thought would never survive?

Those who walk in the Light will act like the Light. They will see the Light. And they will enjoy the Light. Because they know what it was like to live in the darkness.

### PERSONAL TRUTH

*Once you've seen the Light, darkness is not an option.*

### PERSONAL PRAYER

*Jesus, thank you for opening my eyes that I might see and under-*

*stand who you really are. Help me to spend my days helping oth-
ers to find the joy of your Light.*

## PERSONAL QUESTION

*Are there any blind spots in your life?*

# THE GOD WHO
# CONQUERS GIANTS

*We should go up and take possession of the land, for we*
*can certainly do it.*

—Numbers 13:30

Some youth in my Bible study were reenacting the drama of the spies' experiences in the land of Canaan (see Num. 13:27–14:45). In the Bible, Moses delegated the twelve spies, according to God's instructions, to explore the land God had promised them.

The youth divided into two camps: Caleb, from the messianic tribe of Judah, and Joshua, Moses' faithful aide, formed one group. The other ten spies huddled together as group two. Their assignment was to report their findings and convince the remainder of the people to enter in. The remaining of us represented the rest of the two-million-plus Israelites.

The arguments began in heated passion. Caleb argued, "We should go up and take possession. For forty days we examined the potential. See, here is the fruit! It's indeed a land of milk and honey. The people are powerful, and the cities are large and fortified, but we can do it. We can win!"

But the other ten spies spread negative reports. Walking around us, using much exaggeration and many hand gestures, they presented their rebuttal: "Are you kidding? We saw giants—ten feet tall! They would just as soon cut off your head and feed you to the birds! No one could stand against these people. There are too many of them, and we are like grasshoppers in their eyes!"

> We serve a God who can conquer giants!

We played up our part with wails, complaints, and disbelief. "If only we had died in Egypt! We need to choose a new leader and go back. Slavery is better than annihilation!"

The youths portraying Caleb and Joshua interrupted the confusion, pretending to tear their clothes. Two youths assigned as Moses and Aaron fell facedown on the floor and began to pray. "I tell you, we can do it!" pleaded the two positive spies. "We serve a God who can conquer giants! Have you forgotten what he did for us at the Red Sea? If the Lord is with us, we *will* inherit the land!"

Back and forth, like balls in a tennis match, the arguments flew. It appeared the people and negative spies were winning when suddenly, one of the negative spies broke rank and yelled, "Oh, let's just go in!"

The group grew silent, as embarrassed actors do when one of them blows a line or forgets his part. Then bursts of laughter erupted from the entire room.

That's not exactly the way it happened in Scripture. But someone did intervene. God made a personal appearance, so all could see his glory in a cloud. Just when God was about to destroy the entire nation of unbelievers, Moses intervened and begged God to rethink his decision. He appealed to God's reputation. "What will people think? All the nations who have heard of your power will say you couldn't do what you promised."

So God relented and offered a compromise: He would give them the land he had promised; and he would help them conquer the giants. But only Joshua and Caleb—because they had "a different spirit" (Num. 14:24)—would he permit to enter the promised land of Canaan, along with just the descendants of the sinning generation. As a result of the people's unbelief and grumbling against God, a normal two-week trek through the desert turned into a forty-year ordeal—one year for every day the spies explored the land. And the ten spies? God doesn't look favorably on those who spread bad reports. They died of a plague.

The people still didn't believe God. When they attempted to enter and conquer the giants on their own, without God's permission or presence, their new enemies defeated them easily.

I'm sure scores of skeptics didn't believe Terrilee Buxton could conquer the giants of despair, discouragement, and disability, either. Some couldn't, but Terrilee and her mother, Bonnie, had a "different spirit." Terrilee was born without legs and only one arm. For a while, even her mother had difficulty believing Terrilee could defeat her giants. She dreaded how others might treat her daughter.

> Sometimes God surprises us, and in the process, we become good giants of faith.

But Terrilee, who once wore artificial doll legs her grandmother made, proved that those who believe *can* conquer giants. Now a grown woman, she is a wife and mom, "raising her child through an unbending determination to live life as fully as possible." One childhood friend said, "Terrilee can do anything we can do, if not better."

Terrilee herself said she never felt as though she was handicapped: "I never was treated that way, and I can do anything everybody else can." The only thing she says she is not able to do is to play a guitar. But then she never wanted to play a guitar. "There isn't anything I can't do that I want to do."

As for her own baby, Terrilee and her mom called her "the miracle baby"—"because of their belief that their trust in God kept the mother and baby safe." You see, doctors had told Terrilee that some of her medical conditions would complicate her pregnancy and endanger her life—and the baby's. Another giant to conquer. Terrilee did lose one child in pregnancy, but the next one was delivered successfully—a healthy baby boy.[13] I wonder, who was the giant there?

Terrilee proved that God can truly conquer our giants, often by helping us take giant steps of faith. But sometimes God surprises us, and in the process, we become good giants of faith ourselves, like Terrilee.

And Caleb. At age eighty-five, when most men are hobbling with canes, Caleb stood ready in his Nikes and running shorts. He reminded Joshua, who was finally leading the conquest of Canaan, that his forty-year pilgrimage in the desert had only strengthened his resolve and character. He boldly asked for the mountain of Horeb, where the feared Anakites lived—those giants that scared the pants off the ten negative spies years before. How was an eighty-five-year-old senior planning to outwit a mountain full of giants? Did he have a secret battle plan?

Apparently so. When the dust of battle all settled, any visitors to that area discovered that only two giants still remained on Mount Horeb—Caleb and his God.

And both were smiling.

## PERSONAL TRUTH

*Faith is seeing God standing at the top of your mountain, even when you're still struggling in the valley.*

## PERSONAL PRAYER

*God, I cannot handle the giants in my life. I trust you to conquer them one by one. With you, Lord, nothing is impossible.*

## PERSONAL QUESTION

*What giants are you facing?*

DAY 15

# THE OVERPOWERING GOD

*O LORD . . . you overpowered me and prevailed.*
*. . . But if I say, "I will not mention him*
*or speak any more in his name,"*
*his word is in my heart like a fire,*
*a fire shut up in my bones.*

—Jeremiah 20:7, 9

Have you ever been angry at God? Jeremiah was.
Not many would have liked the role God assigned Jeremiah: the prophet of doom. Like an Old Testament John the Baptist, Jeremiah had to warn the people of coming judgment and tell them to repent. Furthermore, God told Jeremiah up front that he would see no change in the people—not in his lifetime. Not too encouraging. Would you say yes if you knew no one would listen or respond to your words?

That, however, didn't seem to be Jeremiah's complaint. He'd just been released from the stocks after enduring another brutal beating for telling the truth. What did he do? He walked right back to the priest who had ordered his flogging in the first place and began to prophesy doom once more.

Then Jeremiah turned aside to God and essentially accused him: "I cannot even shut up if I want to. You are stronger than

I am, God! The truth of your words is like fire out of control—and you won't let any fire extinguisher near me. I try to hold it in, but it's in my bones!"

Like a wildfire spreading through Jeremiah's body, God's message burned deep within his heart, and the prophet felt "overpowered," unable to stop the flames.

> You don't have to wear the name *prophet* to speak truth when truth needs to be told.

We are eager to hear from God when he wants to bless us or to bless people through us. What's the result of an encouraging word or kind act given in God's name? Usually, instant friends. Those God-encounters are the feel-good kind, and God does love to bless his people.

But sometimes God may overpower us with a message that will cut to the quick. You don't have to wear the name *prophet* to speak truth when truth needs to be told. It can happen anywhere: it could be a strong warning to a friend about to plunge headlong into a moral failure; perhaps a lone, dissenting voice at work when integrity is being compromised; or a bold refusal to accept the unhealthy norms of peers. The Bible says, "Faithful are the wounds of a friend; but the kisses of an enemy are deceitful" (Prov. 27:6 KJV). The faithful friend and messenger will speak up, even if the truth hurts.

We can only pray that in those circumstances, because we have such a secure relationship with God, we will cry out, "God, I am not comfortable in this role, but your truth is more powerful and more important than my comfort zone." The results of our refusal to shut up the truth may result in a Jeremiah complex—and no repentance in others around us. But if we allow him to work through us, God can burn our words deep into the hearts of our listeners and bring radical change.

A word of warning: if you find yourself moved to speak up to the ones around you, make sure you are being overpowered by God, and not self. The self-appointed prophet may relish the right to seize authority God never assigned in the first place. Jeremiah never spoke his own thoughts, but God's. He never delivered his own message, but God's. He was compelled to speak because God started the fire.

Loose tongues and proud spirits rush in where even angels fear to tread. The apostle Paul gave ample warning to those willing to accept a divine assignment. Only the "spiritual" ones should help restore others in rebellion. And even then, we are to do so "gently" (Gal. 6:1). Why? God wants us to share his heartbeat and his sorrow over sin. He is always motivated by love and the desire to restore, not condemn. If we do not submit our spirits and our lips to the overpowering God and allow him to burn his love and message deep within our hearts, we leave ourselves wide open to the same temptations and behavior we are warning against. And instead of burning for God, we will burn out quickly.

Many identify Jeremiah not only as the "prophet of doom," but also as the "weeping prophet," because of his deep empathy for God's people (see Jeremiah 9:1). At first glance we would not call his relationship with God joyful. Yet Jeremiah felt comfortable enough with God to vent the full range of his emotions, and God allowed him to do so. Like a gruff army sergeant, for twenty years Jeremiah barked out the harsh

> If God "overpowers" you, speak his words with joyful confidence.

messages from God's mouth to the people of Judah. He grew weary and told God so. He felt depressed enough to die. He hated standing alone—all the time. And his nostrils burned from the smoke of God's overpowering "fire" within him.

Yet Jeremiah kept speaking. Perhaps the reminder of his first encounter with God's presence further explains why Jeremiah couldn't shut up: God had touched Jeremiah's lips and put his words in his mouth. "I am with you," God said (Jer. 1:9). And underneath that gruff exterior, Jeremiah's heart wept for the plight of his people. I believe God wept with him. Jeremiah was not like Jonah, who, after running from God, finally obeyed him and became God's spokesman. Jonah couldn't stand it when the nation of Nineveh believed his words and repented. Bitterness and joy are not compatible bedfellows.

Jeremiah, on the other hand, couldn't stand it because people *refused* to listen, because their hearts *wouldn't* warm to God's words, and because he was so consumed with God that he couldn't do anything else but obey. He was on God's side.

It may not sound like an enjoyable relationship. But I would rather be on God's side, doing what he asks, than choosing my own mission or speaking my own words. Hannah Whitall Smith says, "He who sides with God cannot fail to win every encounter and whether the result shall be joy or sorrow, failure or success, death or life, we may under all circumstances join in the apostles' shout of victory, 'Thanks be unto God, which always causes us to triumph in Christ.'"[14]

If God "overpowers" you, speak his words with joyful confidence. The results are not your issue. The real question is are you willing to be the fire if necessary, or will you draw back, content to be a firefighter?

## PERSONAL TRUTH

*When God overpowers, he will always empower.*

## PERSONAL PRAYER

*Lord, light a fire in my heart and allow the flames to burn brightly for you. Never let me accept comfort over your commission for my life. Break my heart over the spiritual condition and destiny of others. Send me, Lord, wherever you want.*

## PERSONAL QUESTION

*Is there someone God wants you to speak to, or something for which you need to take a stand?*

# THE BRIDEGROOM

*At midnight the cry rang out:*
*"Here's the bridegroom! Come out to meet him!"*
—Matthew 25:6

Anna and Danna both loved boys, pizza, and chocolate. If you looked in both their closets, you would find the same colors: hot pink, green, and black. Both liked shopping, church socials, and volleyball. Everywhere you saw Anna, you knew Danna was close behind. Both wanted to attend college, but needed scholarships to make it financially. Some people thought these two twins were inseparable. In every way, people called them identical. Until something happened in their senior year in high school.

The girls knew that their volleyball performance held the key to their hopes for scholarships. They practiced faithfully and stayed fit throughout the summer prior to their senior year. Both made the starting lineup again and fared well as the team remained undefeated. The local sports writers picked up on their extraordinary skills and touted them as future stars. Visions of scholarships danced in the girls' heads. At any game they knew college scouts could show up looking for future players. And each win played a part in determining their future.

But Danna had formed some new friendships her senior

year, and the two twins began to move apart. The night before the key game, Danna stayed overnight at a friend's house. In a moment of weakness, she yielded to the power of drugs provided by some visiting "friends" of her host. She awoke the next morning feeling confused and listless. When she finally came to her senses, she realized she had only minutes to dress before the big event. But in her haste to make the game in time, Danna turned a corner too quickly. She overcorrected, and the car rammed into a huge oak tree head on.

Danna survived, but her volleyball career didn't. Her injuries ruined her chance for a volleyball scholarship. The college scouts showed up—the night she missed—and later offered her sister Anna a scholarship. Danna's foolishness—and carelessness—cost her a lifelong dream.

> Immediately after the "prenuptial agreement," the bridegroom set to work preparing their future home— often an extension of his own father's house.

In Jesus' story of the ten virgins, another long-awaited day had arrived. Like Danna, five of those virgins made a tragic mistake that would change their lives forever. In this parable, Jesus drew an analogy of himself and the big wedding day of the future.

Ten virgins, five wise and five foolish, waited in anticipation of the big event. Unlike our modern-day customs, Jewish biblical weddings did not set a date for the wedding celebration. Bride and groom were "betrothed" for at least a year—spoken for and sealed with a formal declaration by the two parties in the presence of witnesses. For all purposes, they were considered married, yet they were not allowed to consummate the event until the big day arrived.

Exclusively belonging to one another, each had specific

preparations. The bride kept herself pure, careful to wear her veil of betrothal that said, "I belong to one alone." During this time she also prepared her dowry, her wedding gift to her husband. She was to live in a state of readiness, prepared at any moment for the call to come and her bridegroom to appear and carry her away. Sounds romantic, huh?

Immediately after the "prenuptial agreement," the bridegroom set to work preparing their future home—often an extension of his own father's house. Steadily, patiently, he worked in anticipation of that day when all would be ready. Only his father could conduct the final inspection and declare when the room was ready for the married couple. When the groom received his father's seal of approval, he would then steal away with his attendants, unannounced, often at night—and "capture" his bride.

Together, the entire wedding party would then proceed to the prepared wedding feast and celebration that would sometimes last a week. At the proper time, the wedding couple entered their prepared place and enjoyed the bliss of an intimate love relationship reserved for the married couple alone.

In Jesus' parable, five virgins of the wedding party wisely prepared and waited eagerly with oil in their lamps. At midnight, the call of the shofar trumpet announced, "Here comes the groom!" The virgins had grown sleepy waiting so long, but they rose immediately, grabbing their lamps, eager to join the celebration.

> Our Bridegroom, the Lord Jesus Christ, will come in his full glory at a moment known only to his Father.

The other five virgins, however, had noticed their oil supply was low and probably could not sustain the trip to the wedding feast. They could not beg, borrow, or steal any oil, so in desperation, they dashed to town to try to rouse some sleepy shopkeepers.

But a sad thing happened. While they were gone, the bridegroom arrived. Apparently they had grown lazy and wasted time. Instead of praying, they played. Instead of preparing, they procrastinated—thinking time would stand still for them to regroup and arrive at the last moment. And so they lost their chance to attend the banquet.

The parable stands as a warning to those who would delay the biggest commitment of their lives, but also as an optimistic look into the believer's future. Jesus, our Bridegroom, has gone ahead of us to "prepare a place" (John 14:3). His purpose? Our enjoyment. His reward? Our eternal home.

Our Bridegroom, the Lord Jesus Christ, will come in his full glory at a moment known only to his Father. At that moment, time will not wait for us to go buy oil or wedding garments. If we have prepared our hearts well and have "sealed" the relationship ahead of time with a commitment to him, we will echo eagerly, as if in one huge voice, "Here comes the Bridegroom!" The moment for which we have waited all our lives will arrive, and we will enter the enjoyment of a personal relationship with God forever.

It is not a figment of someone's imagination or a fable, passed on through generations. It is a promise from our heavenly Father and from Jesus, the Bridegroom himself.

It is truly a moment worth waiting for.

## PERSONAL TRUTH

*All of life is a preparation for all of eternity.*

## PERSONAL PRAYER

*Jesus, help me to make wise investments of the time and energy you give me—and to prepare well for your return. Thank you for the precious moments of courtship you give daily, as we walk together in fellowship.*

## PERSONAL QUESTION

*Are you ready to meet the Bridegroom?*

# GOD OF LIFE AND DEATH

*When the body touched Elisha's bones,*
*the man came to life and stood up on his feet.*

—2 Kings 13:21

The mighty man of God, Elisha, spent years serving him: healing, teaching, prophesying, and ministering to kings. Then came his time to die. God did not heal him of his illness, and he died.

It was the end of Elisha and his power—a legend in his own time. Remember, he was not transfigured like Elijah. Yet death did not eradicate the power and anointing of God—even on his dead bones.

We are not told the purpose of this account. Some Moabite raiders entering Israel every spring, looking for an easy target, stumbled upon some Israelites burying a dead man. Terrorized by the band of raiders, the Israelites fled for their lives, hastily throwing the unburied body into the nearest tomb—which just happened to be Elisha's burial place.

What happened next could be additional fodder for the old spiritual about "them dry bones" coming to life. For what reason? Did the men stick around to see it happen? (Can you imagine the shock of witnessing such an event?) Did the raiders stumble onto the tomb about the time the dead man jumped out of the grave? Did Elijah's mantle also lie buried in the tomb beside the prophet's bones? If so, could the dead man have touched that powerful mantle as well?

Someone witnessed the supernatural occurrence and lived to record it. You can bet a story like that made the rounds and caused great fear of the Israelites' powerful God.

> Death didn't stop the powerful effect of a dead man on the lives of others.

What was the purpose of such a spectacle? Was it to glorify the man, the servant Elisha—to prove once again what a powerful man of God he was? Perhaps not. If we look closely, we will see once again a passage that points not to a man's miraculous power, but to the awesome, supernatural power of a holy God. It was not Elisha's power that restored the dead man, but the same powerful Spirit that had anointed Elisha in his lifetime.

Death didn't stop the powerful effect of a dead man on the lives of others. Can you imagine the shock of the man who was instantly resurrected? I imagine he was never the same again.

God is the God of Life and Death. Have you ever heard a preacher exhort the mourners at a funeral with these words: "We often touch more people in our deaths than in our lifetimes"? Often, the sudden, tragic death of a dear believer—or nonbeliever—sobers those who witness the event, and they realize for the first time their mortality, their need for God, and his power to change their lives.

Bart Millard, multiple Dove Award winner and lead singer/composer of Mercy Me, can testify to this truth. At the sudden and tragic death of his wife's twenty-year-old brother, Bart took the opportunity to address those attending the funeral. In the packed auditorium, amidst the tears and heartache, Bart's words targeted primarily a small group of mourners—fellow friends and classmates of the deceased. "If you want to do something for Chris," he spoke boldly, "get your life right with God."

And many of them did. Death had stolen a life prematurely, but that day some happened to stumble onto the awesome resurrection power of a holy God. It was not Chris's life that changed them, or even his death. God took the remains of tragedy and turned it into an opportunity to glorify himself—and to bring new life into his kingdom of believers.

God is indeed the God of Life and Death. Suppose the one who dies has truly been a powerful witness for God. We may wonder why such a saint, who really seemed to be making a difference, is cut down early in life, like a young tree robbed of its best years of fruitfulness. In God's scheme of things, perhaps some "dying" soul may one day stumble upon the skeleton of that person's life—his words, his teachings, his testimony, his godly legacy—and God's power will touch a spiritual nerve.

> God took the remains of tragedy and turned it into an opportunity to glorify himself—and to bring new life into his kingdom of believers.

Perhaps there is more behind Paul's statement: "He who began a good work in you will carry it on to completion until the day of Christ Jesus" (Phil. 1:6). The Bible doesn't say God will complete the work in us until our death, but that he will continue the good work until Christ comes. That means death doesn't necessarily end God's purposes in our lives. In fact, sometimes, that's just when he's getting started.

One person dies, but not in vain. Another one lives to take

up the mantle and story and begins to spread the news: "You, too, can know and enjoy this awesome God! Just look what he has done in my life!"

### PERSONAL TRUTH

*Dead men may tell no tales, but their message lives on to preach powerful sermons.*

### PERSONAL PRAYER

*Lord, let me so live that when I die, your power will live on in others. Help me to take up the mantle of those gone before me and use every opportunity to birth new life into your kingdom.*

### PERSONAL QUESTION

*If your life were a book, what would someone read in it?*

# THE KING, THE LORD ALMIGHTY

*"Woe to me!" I cried. "I am ruined!*
*For I am a man of unclean lips,*
*and I live among a people of unclean lips,*
*and my eyes have seen the King, the LORD Almighty."*

—Isaiah 6:5

God's revelations of himself are not always as dramatic as his call to Isaiah. But when God is about to do a great work, he often uses a spectacular mode of communication. We can only speculate why. Perhaps some of God's purposes are to make sure the recipient knows God means business, to convince the person of who God is and that he is capable of carrying out his plans.

When God's glory, the "train of his robe," filled the temple, he spared no use of visual Technicolor; Isaiah saw in his vision or encounter the "Lord, high and exalted." Seraphs—otherworldly beings defined as "something burning and dazzling"—hovered above God's throne. And the music they sang was like no choir Isaiah had ever heard! Attesting to God's awesome character, they half shouted, half sang to one another, "Holy, holy, holy is the LORD Almighty" (Isa. 6:1, 3).

Isaiah was not the only one shaking in his sandals at the sound of these voices. The noise and God's presence were so powerful that the doorposts and thresholds shook, and the entire temple smelled as if it were on fire.

> Immediately the purity and holiness of a perfect God shone the light on the human weakness and sinfulness of a mere man.

What a penetrating cry from Isaiah when he realized he stood in the presence of the Almighty. If truly no one could see God and live, then Isaiah knew he was facing destruction (see Exodus 33:20). Immediately the purity and holiness of a perfect God shone the light on the human weakness and sinfulness of a mere man. And Isaiah cried out, "I am ruined! My lips are unclean!" He knew sin and God didn't mix. And Isaiah at once recognized he literally could not stand in the presence of a holy God as he was and live. None of us could either.

But this almighty God *wanted* Isaiah to live. So with tongs from the altar of God's presence, a seraph touched Isaiah's lips with live coals and burned away the sinfulness and guilt in his life. His sins were "atoned for" (Isa. 6:7).

The triune God could then use the man as his messenger. He had touched Isaiah personally and prepared him to take a key role in warning his people to return to him. But God also assigned Isaiah the privilege of prophesying, hundreds of years before its fulfillment, the coming of Christ—the world's true salvation.

"Whom shall I send?" God thundered to Isaiah. "And who will go for us?" And Isaiah was compelled to speak boldly with an enthusiastic, "I will! I will! Here am I! Send me!" (see Isa. 6:8).

What makes the difference in the messenger who speaks from his own heart and the one who declares bold truth from God's heart? The difference is the anointing touch of God upon a life. The difference is in the one who has allowed God to burn away his sin and replace it with God's own fiery brand of purity.

Some people may think that holiness and purity are mystical attributes reserved for priestly prophets like Isaiah. Martin Luther said, "Holiness consisteth not in a cowl or in a garment of gray—when God purifies the heart by faith, the market is sacred as well as the sanctuary; neither remaineth there any work or place which is profane."[15]

Iris and Duane Blue lived anything but priestly lives when God touched them and radically changed their lives. I first heard Iris's testimony years ago and was impressed by her dramatic testimony and the authenticity of her life.

Iris dreamed of being a lady—wonderful and feminine. But she thought being a lady was about looks, and Iris was big, towering over boys in her class. Awkward, discouraged, and bent on finding freedom, Iris ran away from home. By the time she was fourteen, she was a heroin addict, thief, and prostitute, working in a topless bar. Iris says, "I was a lady all right—a lady of the night."

Iris continued her downward spiral and spent seven years in prison for armed robbery. But even prison didn't change her. Some time later Iris's aunt agreed to help sew dresses for her girls' opening night at one of her topless clubs—only if Iris would agree to attend church with her. She did, and God planned a divine encounter for Iris. A man from

> Only when we admit our nothingness will we experience God's holy touch on our lives.

that church refused to give up on showing God's love to her. He came to her strip club repeatedly to witness to her, even when Iris tried to "mess him up by putting dope in his food" and tempt him with "some of the 'house specials.'" Finally, God intervened and Iris knelt on the ground in front of her topless bar and asked God to take over her life. Iris says, "That night I got out of the bar business."

Jesus changed her life that night, and burned away her past. Like Isaiah, her life could now radiate the holiness of God. She later met Duane, whose past was equally shocking. The two later married. Infused with a divine boldness, they, too, answered God's call with "Here we are! Send us!" Both now serve as Mission Service Corps volunteers, and they freely share their life-changing encounter with the King, the Lord Almighty.[16]

Casual messages will fall on shallow, unfertile hearts unless the messenger has encountered the living God. Only when we admit our nothingness will we experience God's holy touch on our lives. And when we see his awesome holiness with new eyes and clean hearts, we will enjoy a personal relationship with God that demands both expression and service. At that point we will not be able to keep now-clean lips from shouting joyfully, "Holy, holy, holy is the Lord God Almighty! Send *me*, Lord! *Please* send *me*!"

## PERSONAL TRUTH

*The fires of revival often begin when one person is willing to be a living flame for God.*

## PERSONAL PRAYER

*Holy God, I have nothing to offer except a willing heart and life.*

*Purify my lips that I might be your spokesperson in this generation.*
*Let them see the fires of your love in the flames of my heart.*

## PERSONAL QUESTION

*Does God need to "burn away" anything from your life?*

# THE GOD IN HEAVEN ABOVE AND ON THE EARTH BELOW

*When we heard of it, our hearts melted*
*and everyone's courage failed because of you,*
*for the LORD your God is God in heaven above*
*and on the earth below.*

—Joshua 2:11

Moses had died. Joshua's time to enter the promised land had finally come. An entire unbelieving generation, including the ten negative spies who first reported victory as impossible years earlier, had passed from the scene. As one of the two believing spies, Joshua had made a positive report to Moses. Armed with the promise of God and a godly mentor's lessons, Joshua then sent in only two spies to help them visualize their action plan to conquer the land. "Go, look over the land," he said, "especially Jericho" (Josh. 2:1). The spies took refuge at the house of a prostitute named Rahab.

Wary eyes were always watching, however, and the king of Jericho got wind of the spies' visit. He sent a message to Rahab to surrender the men. But Rahab had already conceived a plan. She hid the men, then told a lie to cover up their presence.

What caused Rahab to risk her life for two strangers? Why didn't the fear of the king's wrath motivate her to expose the men for who they were? Where did she find such courage?

God's reputation had preceded Joshua's visit. Jericho's inhabitants had heard of the Israelites' unbelievable exodus through the Red Sea. Then word spread of how they had already begun defeating their new enemies. People recognized this was no ordinary feat, and certainly not one their gods could perform.

> God had a bigger picture in mind. He always does.

We are not told how many really heard of this miraculous God and believed. But Rahab did. The fear of Joshua's God had struck a chord in Rahab's heart, and her simple faith in the God in Heaven Above and on the Earth Below superseded all the other "gods" she may have previously embraced. She recognized that belief in this God could save her and her family from death—both from the king, and from this superior God—when Joshua's men moved in to destroy the city of Jericho.

Rahab's valiant actions so stirred God's heart that she earned a place in the roll call of heroes in the book of Hebrews' Hall of Faith (Heb. 11:31). From that point on, Rahab was known as a woman of faith and was spared the destruction of those around her when the walls of Jericho fell. God could have chosen a ho-hum method for the Israelite people to cross to their promised land. All the time, those Israelites might have thought that miraculous Red Sea crossing was for their benefit alone. Not so. God had a bigger picture in mind. He always does.

The two spies told Rahab to gather her family members together in the house and tie a scarlet cord in the window, in order to guarantee her rescue when Joshua's army entered the city. The two men agreed to spare her life under those conditions. Then they headed out to the hills, where they hid for three days. Their words to Joshua upon their return from spying the land: "The LORD has surely given the whole land into our hands; all the people are melting in fear because of us" (Josh. 2:24).

The scarlet cord, a foreshadowing of events to come generations later, points to the ultimate bigger picture for all time. The God in Heaven Above and on the Earth Below devised his plan of action long before the foundation of the world. And there, at Rahab's window, was the invitation that would continue to be heard around the world for all time: Jesus, the scarlet thread of Christianity, is woven throughout the Bible and documented history. The scarlet thread led to Bethlehem and Calvary, where God's big picture was completed. Jesus' "scarlet" blood would provide the "window" and guarantee of escape from every person's spiritual death.

You may think supernatural happenings around you are simply coincidences, or that they occur because of your or someone else's genius. And if you do recognize a miracle for what it truly is, you might think God actually did it just for you. And he did—because that's the kind of God he is. But be careful that you don't miss the bigger picture as well.

> The God in Heaven Above and on the Earth Below devised his plan of action long before the foundation of the world.

Whether God reveals himself today in the miraculous or the ordinary is not the issue. That he reveals himself at all is so that all generations (yours included) will know his reputation and character—so that the holy, reverent, awesome, powerful, fearful name of God will overpower the "gods" we humans often embrace; so that he will draw us to himself. God wants all people, even the Rahabs of the world, to know he is the one true God: the God in Heaven Above and on the Earth Below, and the only one who can meet our deepest needs.

The fear of the Lord is the beginning place for enjoying his wisdom—and a starting place to know and enjoy him personally.

## Personal Truth

*A miracle is always a God-incident.*

## Personal Prayer

*God, help me to see everything that happens in light of eternity. When my world is too small, help me to grasp the bigger picture. But thank you that you are a personal God who loves to meet my needs as well.*

## Personal Question

*Have you experienced any God-incidents lately?*

# THE LORD OF THE HARVEST

*However, do not rejoice that the spirits submit to you,*
*but rejoice that your names are written in heaven.*

—Luke 10:20

Jesus was ready to empower more disciples, perhaps to let his twelve know that they were not alone—God can and will empower whom he wants. Jesus saw a world desperately in need of peace, hope, and purpose. He knew his death and resurrection would provide these for all who sought him, and his three-year mission would convince many followers. After his death, many laborers would be needed to carry on his work. He chose to use people touching other people.

So Jesus gave seventy-two willing followers the assignment of working on the harvest. They would be like lambs among wolves. Their reception might be less than pleasant—wolves chew up lambs and spit out the bones.

Jesus instructed the followers not to be distracted on their mission; they should take no money for side trips to the Bass Pro Shop or outlet malls, not even an extra pair of shoes, camping gear, or an overnight bag. He told them not to spend time greeting travelers with traditional small talk, which could last for hours. Jesus wanted them to remember their mission, to stay focused on their purpose. The main harvest would come where the people were—in their towns.

The primary message: "The kingdom of God is near" (Luke 10:9). The unwritten rest of the message: "Prepare—and believe in the one who can open the gate to eternal life." Jesus reminded his followers that those who rejected them also rejected him, and those who accepted their words also accepted him.

> The main harvest would come where the people were— in their towns.

The message of those laborers in God's harvest was simple and straightforward. They handed out no scarlet cords to hang from the windows of believers' homes, and they did not recommend that people sprinkle blood on their doorposts for an angel to see as God passed over.

In Jesus' instructions to his followers, he revealed the kind of power he would give them: "Heal the sick who are there" (Luke 10:9). In other words, "Where there are needs, I am giving you the power to meet those needs." Jesus knew people had a tendency to believe when miraculous power authenticated the message. And he, the Lord of the Harvest, wanted to make sure his disciples understood that power came from God alone.

The seventy-two returned, enamored with the power. The first words out of their mouths were not "Lord, what a wonder you are! Truly you are the Son of God! We are in awe of who you are!" Instead, they cried out, "Lord, even the demons submit to us in your name" (Luke 10:17).

Their comments prompted Jesus to offer his swift warning. Jesus had witnessed the worst-case scenario of pride: in a moment of weakness, filled with the exhilaration of heavenly power, Satan wanted it all. He wanted equality with God. Jesus had seen his Father's swift retribution for Satan's rebellion as he hurled the fallen angel and his misplaced pride to the ground like a swift bolt of lightning.

We see it happen all the time. A messenger is called out to the harvest, gifted beyond his or her own abilities, empowered to do good things for God. Scores follow, lives are radically changed, and people are even healed of lifelong habits and illnesses.

And then soon after, we read the newspaper headlines. Another disciple "fell from heaven" like lightning gone amok, causing havoc wherever it struck.

Some will indeed find their way back in humility and usefulness again, because God truly wants to restore, but others will fail to see the problem. Like the fallen angel Satan, they may cry out, "Look at me! Even demons bow to me!" Like Satan, they lust for more power.

At least the seventy-two recognized their power came from the name of Jesus. Jesus also knew, however, the tendency of every man and woman given a great assignment and the accompanying power with which to accomplish it. Those disciples did not return humbled by seeing people turn from death to life. They did not come back sharing the miracles of people's lives changed from darkness to light. They did not acknowledge that they were unworthy of the assignment, that truly, the harvest was great, or cry as Isaiah might, "Lord, send me again . . . and again . . . and again."

> And he, the Lord of the Harvest, wanted to make sure his disciples understood that power came from God alone.

But like a tender father with a small child, Jesus exhorted his followers, "Do not rejoice that the spirits submit to you. Rejoice that your names are written in heaven." In other words, "Don't rejoice in the power. Find joy solely in our relationship. Let your joy be in me!"

It was a caution God gave even back in Old Testament times:

> *But let him who boasts, boast about this:*
> *that he understands and knows me,*
> *that I am the LORD, who exercises kindness,*
> *justice and righteousness on earth,*
> *for in these I delight.* (Jeremiah 9:24)

When we find joy in Jesus alone, we will have no other reason to boast, and we will need nothing else to satisfy—no miracles, no blessings, no signs from heaven. Anything else God grants is a fringe benefit and a gift to offer back to him.

### PERSONAL TRUTH

*Seizing the day never means seizing the power.*

### PERSONAL PRAYER

*Lord, whatever you give to me in this journey is unimportant. If you do not go before me; if you do not go with me; if you are not the heartbeat behind every word, thought, or action, I am useless. Help me find my joy in you, and in you alone.*

### PERSONAL QUESTION

*How do you feel when you have completed an assignment from God?*

# The God Who Brings Discernment

*When they got up early in the morning,*
*the sun was shining on the water.*
*To the Moabites across the way,*
*the water looked red—like blood.*

—2 Kings 3:22

Three kings—of Israel, Judah, and Edom—united for battle against the king of Moab. Parched after a seven-day march, they faced a crisis in the desert: no water for their armies or their animals. One of the king's officers had heard of the prophet Elisha's miracle-making power. They decided to seek Elisha's counsel and help.

Elisha finally agreed. He received a word from the Lord: "Dig ditches all over this valley. Here's what will happen—you won't hear the wind, you won't see the rain, but this valley is going to fill up with water and your army and your animals will drink their fill. This is easy for GOD to do; he will also hand Moab over to you" (2 Kings 3:16–18 MSG). An amazing promise. But sure enough; the next morning, about the time of the morning sacrifice, the dry land turned into a virtual lake.

The Moabites had heard rumors of war, so they had prepared for battle. When they arose early the next morning, however, they looked out over the valley and saw an unusual sight. The golden sun's reflection made the water appear red like blood. The king of Moab and his men immediately assumed their enemy armies had fought each other instead and that what remained was a bloody mess. Great lust filled their hearts as they set out like vultures to scarf up the dead's bounty.

> The hidden snares of sudden wealth or what looks like easy plunder too often prove a trap to the ones who see with only temporal eyes.

The Israelites awoke early that morning as well, prepared to see God's promise fulfilled. And God did not disappoint them. When the Moabites strutted into the camp of Israel, they learned too late that things are not always as they appear. The Israelite army met them head-on with a surprise attack and slaughtered them as they chased them all the way back into their own land of Moab. And then, just as God instructed, the Israelites "stopped up all the springs and cut down every good tree" and "threw a stone on every good field until it was covered" (2 Kings 3:25).

The same thing could happen to us. All that glitters is not necessarily gold—or red, in this case. The hidden snares of sudden wealth or what looks like easy plunder too often prove a trap to the ones who see with only temporal eyes. Once the fingers touch the forbidden object of their pursuit, the glitter is transformed before their very eyes. And as with King Midas, the plan backfires, leaving lifeless, unusable stones of regret: defeated lives and often empty bank accounts.

According to an IFCC Internet Fraud Report, the FBI reports thousands of fraud claims each year from unsuspecting victims who have discovered things are not always as they appear. In 2002, those claims rose sharply and tripled from a year earlier.[17] Scambusters.org, a Web site by Audri and Jim Lanford, lists scores of frauds. Their general rule is that tried-and-true adage, "If it sounds too good to be true, it probably is."

One of the most common scams they list is the work-at-home E-mail, ad, or letter that promises big bucks for little work. These scams usually try to mooch off the sick, disabled, elderly, and low-income or no-income persons. The proposed business opportunities range from craft assembly, E-mail processing, calling 1-900 numbers for more information (which costs money), envelope stuffing, chain letters, and home typing jobs. Most require an investment and research that could involve more hours and much more money than originally promised.[18]

One of Scambusters' newsletters tells about a scam that has been around for years. It involves an overseas letter that targets "small- and medium-sized businesses, as well as charities." The letter comes from someone claiming to be a worker from that nation's bank or government. That "senior civil servant" is looking for an honest foreign company where he can transfer some funds overpaid by his nation's government. The amount listed can range in the millions. Other false documents and letters may accompany the offer. Because this involves the government, they claim they cannot "operate a foreign account."

The victim thinks, "Wow! I am so lucky they picked me!" But once he has agreed to the terms of the offer, the sometimes-threatening pressure begins. Suddenly large sums

> God gives counsel to the pure in heart.

of money are needed from the victim to protect and "save the venture"—before the money can even be transferred. More and more demands may come, but not before the victim is bilked of huge sums.[19]

The FBI reports that millions of dollars are scammed from American citizens each year.[20] Why? In some cases, such as the overseas scheme, the victims start to see themselves with the money and feel all the ways it will change their lives.[21] In other fraudulent offers, the victim may simply be visualizing the fulfillment of a long-time dream or be driven by desperation and hopeless circumstances. Like the Moabites, the potential victims see the reflection of the sun on the water and think, "This is a cinch. The bounty is as good as mine."

God gives counsel to the pure in heart. The one who searches for his ways will not be deceived when tempted by fool's gold—empty pursuits or treasures that shine from sin's reflections. Only those who listen well will truly discern that beneath that mirage of apparent easy gold lies a pool of actual blood, streaming from the destruction of others who walked temptation's path before them and were defeated.

Only those who learn to see through God's eyes can truly enjoy the God Who Brings Discernment. And if that sounds too good to be true, you really *can* believe it with confidence. God's instructions and promises never fail.

### Personal Truth

*Seeing is believing—God's truth.*

### Personal Prayer

*Lord, give us eyes to see what you see and hearts that discern good from evil. Grant us safety from danger, and help us set our affections on you and you alone!*

### Personal Question

*What mistakes have you learned from?*

# THE GOD OF ALL COMFORT

*Praise be to the . . . Father of compassion and the God of all comfort,*
*who comforts us in all our troubles,*
*so that we can comfort those in any troubles*
*with the comfort we ourselves have received from God.*

—2 Corinthians 1:3-4

Gerald Mann thought he knew the true meaning of comfort. After all, as pastor of Riverbend Church in Austin, Texas, he had empathized with and come alongside thousands of people in tragedies and losses. "I thought I knew what it was like to lose a mate because I had been with so many people who had," said Mann. But he discovered that to truly give comfort, one must first be comforted himself.

Sometimes it's the healer who needs the healing. Several years ago, Mann lost his wife, Lois, after a series of heart surgeries. They had walked together, comforting others, for forty-two years. Then it was Pastor Mann who was in need of comfort.

Mann's congregation must have understood God's principle of comforting others. Through the years, in the midnight hours, on holidays, at the bedsides of loved ones, in emergency rooms, and in the marriage counseling office, they had felt the arms of God around their shoulders through the soothing words and expressions of their pastor. Now it was their turn.

Seeing Pastor Mann's need, some close friends invited him on a "healing mission" to Africa, where he and his wife had worked years earlier—only the healing was for Pastor Mann. As he walked back through the memories and revisited the places he and his wife had seen, Mann took the time and the freedom to grieve—and found the comforting hand of God in a way he had perhaps never experienced.

> He wants us to know he understands where we are.

And at home, scores of cards and international letters flooded Mann's mailbox, the writers extending the same comfort with which they had been comforted for so long. Three weeks after his wife died, Mann had apologized for his lack of understanding. But how could he have known the depth of their sorrow? According to all his friends' notes and expressions, which ministered to him greatly, God still used Mann to comfort them in their distress before his own tragedy.[22] How much more Mann could now empathize with them and others after feeling the grace of God comforting him. In the months to follow, as the pastor spent precious time reflecting, no doubt his relationship would grow even deeper with God after experiencing the God of All Comfort himself.

Mildred Tengbom says, "Reflecting on how our loss has affected our relationship to God can enrich us spiritually. Have we experienced more fully our need for the God who saves and forgives? Have we known in a new way His faithfulness, felt comforted by His understanding and been warmed by His love? . . . If such changes have taken place, then our loss has enriched us spiritually."[23]

God has many purposes for tragedy. To try and figure them all out will only leave us exhausted and confused. But one reason God makes perfectly clear: he wants us to know he understands where we are. "Surely he took up our infirmities and carried our sorrows, / yet we considered him stricken by God, / smitten by him, and afflicted" (Isa. 53:4). God knows personally what it is like to grieve, to suffer loss. The difference is that he did it willingly—so we could experience his authentic comfort. God suffered the loss of his own Son to prove he is the loving God of All Comfort (John 3:16).

When the disciples were grieving the earthly loss of their Master and Teacher, Jesus was busy comforting them, first with his reassuring appearance after his resurrection, then through his gift: the Comforter, the Holy Spirit.

The disciples in turn, having been comforted, extended the work of the Comforter. So did Paul. In all his troubles, imprisonments, and losses, Paul said, "Just as the sufferings of Christ flow over into our lives, so also through Christ our comfort overflows. If we are distressed, it is for your comfort" (2 Cor. 2:5-6). The Holy Spirit strengthened all of them and enabled them to bring healing, hope, and restoration to the blind, the lame, and the sick. God allowed Paul to use words of exhortation and comfort in his many letters to the churches he had visited. Each time we read of their experiences and see how the Spirit enabled them to keep serving, to care about others' needs, and to look beyond their distress even in the midst of such trying times, we are encouraged to do the same.

> God suffered the loss of his own Son to prove he is the loving God of All Comfort.

Larry and I learned that well when, fifteen years into our marriage, we experienced some rocky times. But with hard work, determined love, and God's tender help and comfort, we discovered the joys of our relationship were worth fighting for. We learned what love could really mean. In the years following, God placed a desire in our hearts to pass on his comfort by encouraging other couples. We trained as marriage enrichment leaders and began to lead couple retreats so we could help strengthen others and help them prevent problems in areas such as communication and conflict resolution. Together we have experienced the privilege of sharing with scores of couples the truths we came to learn ourselves. Without having experienced difficulty and the accompanying comfort God brings through it, we may have good intentions, but our lighthearted attempts at comforting others could be misinterpreted. The Bible says, "Singing light songs to the heavyhearted is like pouring salt in their wounds" (Prov. 25:20 MSG). At those times perhaps the best thing we can do is to weep with those who weep. We can do what Job's friends did when they first heard of his great losses: they simply sat with him in silence for seven days. It was later, when then they tried to open their mouths and speak of things they knew nothing about, that they got into trouble.

I remember my first year in college when one of the girls on my dorm floor had lost a grandmother. Up until that time I had experienced few losses in my family. No appropriate words came to mind—only phrases I had heard others say. So I grabbed my ukulele and just sat in her room playing lighthearted songs. Months later when I lost my own grandmother, and years later, my own father, I realized the foolishness of such an action, and my responses changed to heartfelt empathy. It was only when I experienced a loved one's death that I understood how sorrow could pierce the heart—and how the comfort of God and others could help heal it.

If you must say something, "I can't imagine what you are going through, but I hurt for you" may be the most well-received words you can offer to someone in the midst of adversity, especially if you haven't walked in their shoes.

Tragedy is a given. We will all experience it sometime in our lives. We know that genuine healing and joy have returned when we are truly able to pass on the miraculous work of the God of All Comfort—the one who has personally comforted us—by coming alongside of and comforting others, holding their hands and hearts gently as they heal.

Just ask Gerald Mann.

### PERSONAL TRUTH

*Those who experience and enjoy God's comfort will never lack for friends.*

### PERSONAL PRAYER

*Lord, thank you for all the times you have comforted me in my losses and difficulties. And thank you for allowing me the privilege of knowing what suffering is like, so I can pass on your sweet comfort to someone else who needs it.*

### PERSONAL QUESTION

*How has God allowed you to comfort someone else?*

# THE HIGH AND LOFTY ONE

*I live in a high and holy place,*
*but also with him who is contrite and lowly in spirit.*

—Isaiah 57:15

I n Bible times, kings did not usually mix with the lowly. Living in palatial structures, they surrounded themselves with well-known dignitaries, wealthy friends, and respected leaders in their kingdoms. To fellowship with ordinary riffraff was beneath their dignity.

So high and lofty were kings in Queen Esther's day, even she could not approach the throne of her husband without permission. To do so could mean instant death. Only if the king extended a golden scepter to her could Esther go into his presence. Everyone treated the king as "high and lofty"— someone to be feared.

Yet Isaiah spoke of a different kind of king: one who indeed lives in a high and holy place, one who will live forever—whose very name means "holy." This kind of king voluntarily removes the obstacles between laity and royalty.

This kind of king welcomes the "contrite and lowly in spirit." This does not necessarily mean the down-and-out, although our King does open his throne to those. He does not define *lowly* as the helpless, though he pays attention to those.

Rather, the contrite and lowly in spirit are the ones who have voluntarily humbled themselves, or whose sin has broken them. They are the ones who have experienced disaster and discouragement through their circumstances but who have returned to God with hearts eager to obey. They are the ones who have learned to view sin as God does.

> This kind of king welcomes the "contrite and lowly in spirit."

This kind of king offers a promise: "I have seen his ways [his sin]; but I will heal him; / I will guide him and restore comfort to him, / creating praise on the lips of the mourners in Israel" (Isa. 57:18–19).

The Bible tells about another person in a high position who once demonstrated this same character. David had made a covenant with Jonathan, his friend and the son of King Saul, in which he promised never to cut off his kindness from Saul's family (see 1 Sam. 20:14–15, 17). Saul turned against David, pursuing him relentlessly in fits of jealous rage. David eventually took over the throne, and Saul died in battle. But the war between the house of Saul and the house of David continued for years.

When the fighting finally subsided, and most of Saul's family were killed, including Jonathan, David asked a strange question about his enemy: "Is there anyone still left of the house of Saul to whom I can show kindness for Jonathan's sake?" (2 Sam. 9:1).

Someone located a servant of Saul named Ziba and questioned him. Saul still had one living relative: Jonathan's crippled son, Mephibosheth. When this young man hobbled into David's presence, he immediately fell at David's feet, fearful for his life. But David, the high and lofty king, offered grace and mercy to the grandson of his worst enemy. Not only did he restore to Jonathan's son all the land that previously belonged to Saul, but then he pointed to his own royal table and said to Mephibosheth, "Furthermore, from now on you'll take all your meals at my table."

Then, "shuffling and stammering, not looking him in the eye, Mephibosheth said, 'Who am I that you pay attention to a stray dog like me?'" (2 Sam. 9:7–8 MSG).

David even showed generosity to Ziba's family and servants and Mephibosheth's young son—over thirty-five people in all. He wanted not to harm them, but to show kindness.

What kind of royalty can you think of whose passion is to restore worth and dignity to the lowliest person? What kind of king extends the royal scepter of his heart, who declares the way open for all to approach? What kind of king stretches his arms wide in love to the very subjects who have betrayed him, disobeyed him, and even hated him?

This kind of king is none other than God himself—and he is never too high or lofty to reach down to embrace sinful men and women: to heal, restore, and bless with joy and peace.

> What kind of royalty can you think of whose passion is to restore worth and dignity to the lowliest person?

To those who are willing to receive, to the very ones who have despised him, the High and Lofty God says, "Come back to me. I forgive you, and I love you. I want you to know me personally. I want you to enjoy sweet fellowship with me. My kingdom is your kingdom. My home is your home. Come and dine at my table."

This king does not select just a few friends in high places. He invites everyone, including you and me. He has not prepared leftovers, but a sumptuous feast. He will not send us to the servant's quarter for our meals. He will not keep us waiting at the front door. We don't have to shuffle or stammer or shrink from fear in his presence. He doesn't care what we look like; he loves us exactly as we are. No matter where we have been, or what we have done, our King says, "Please, come. I will be here waiting for you."

It's an offer too good to refuse.

## PERSONAL TRUTH

*The sign above God's royal throne always reads "Welcome."*

## PERSONAL PRAYER

*Lord, I receive your offer joyfully. Thank you for extending your royal scepter of love and grace to one such as me.*

## PERSONAL QUESTION

*How has the High and Lofty One made you feel welcome?*

DAY 24

# THE LIVING MANNA

# FROM HEAVEN

*Again Jesus said, "Simon son of John,*
*do you truly love me?*
*. . . Feed my sheep."*

—John 21:16–17

Following his resurrection, Jesus was about to ascend back to his Father. But first he made one more appearance to the disciples, especially to Peter. His words to Peter were not "I told you so!" or "Peter, why did you deny me? Couldn't you have at least been faithful to me at my death?" Jesus knows we cannot enjoy or love him passionately until we have been freed from and forgiven for our past.

Jesus did not remind Peter of his mistakes but challenged him to move on. He repeated his original call to him: "Follow me" ( John 21:19). And he gave Peter another job to do—not a meaningless, busy activity in which Peter could lose himself or quell his grief and regret, but an important assignment. Jesus examined the disciple's love and devotion for him, then offered him another chance, another test: "If you really love me, Peter, feed my sheep." In other words, "Let your love for me drive you to give others food—the same food with which I have fed you."

Perhaps Peter's mind flashed back to one day on the Judean hillside. Jesus had been teaching all day to multitudes of eager listeners. They were all tired and hungry, and the disciples begged Jesus to urge the people to leave and find food and lodging. Peter remembered his Master's words to the disciples: "You give them something to eat" (Luke 9:13).

> "Let your love for me drive you to give others food— the same food with which I have fed you."

The disciples stared at each other in disbelief. *He doesn't get it*, they were thinking. Five thousand hungry men, *plus* women and children had to be fed. Where would they get enough food to feed such a crowd?

One of the disciples saw a young boy with a very small lunch basket. *Surely this will convince Jesus that we need more— much more—food*, the disciples thought. They said, "We have only five loaves of bread and two fish unless we go and buy food for all this crowd" (Luke 9:13).

But to him who rained manna and quail from heaven to feed hundreds of thousands in the desert, this was not a problem, but another opportunity and wonderful object lesson for the disciples. After blessing the pitiful lunch, Jesus took the food and began breaking—and breaking and breaking—the bread and fish. When all the people had eaten, twelve basketsful of leftovers remained.

Jesus was still challenging the disciples' faith. His words to Peter, "Feed my sheep," did not mean "Find five loaves and two fishes and duplicate my miracle." That could happen, but perhaps Jesus was simply saying, "My sheep are starving for love, for peace, for joy, for purpose, for eternal life. Go, feed them. I have given you the food you need—my living manna from heaven. You have eaten of this manna. You know where it comes from."

Peter's passionate affection for Jesus would eventually grow into a mature love. Sometimes that happens as we simply go and obey and God stirs up in our hearts a new love for his lambs. Sometimes he removes the scales of our spiritually blind eyes and lets us see the tremendous needs of people—his sheep. And always it occurs when, like Peter at Pentecost, we wait with faith and abandonment and allow his Spirit to fill us with his power. When he does, the manifestations of that power may catch us by surprise at times.

That's what happened to me not long ago as I was leading a women's retreat. A woman approached me before the session began and asked if I would come with her so she could pray for me. As we prayed together, she spoke boldly with great passion and asked God to take over and give me freedom to deliver his living manna. When this prayer warrior finished, our spirits agreed in desiring that God's presence would spill over into the meeting room and touch many lives.

God answered those prayers and gave me freedom to speak my heart. Then as I was singing a song at the end, I felt as if God had ripped away an invisible curtain and allowed me to see not just the outside of women's faces, but inside their hearts where needs and hurts lay exposed. Like a fountain bubbling up inside, tears began to trickle down my cheeks and onto the floor. My fingers were flying, but my heart was crying. God *loved* these women. Did they really understand how much? Did I?

Some did, for several women cornered me afterwards in

> If we know Jesus, we possess manna that will never run out, never dry up, and never grow stale.

private consultations. I left that afternoon, more aware than ever that God's words are indeed powerful, that his sheep are hungry, and that he wants us as his disciples, to faithfully feed them.

Jesus did not give Peter, or us, crumbs with which to feed his sheep, but the seed of agape—love—a seed that would emerge from the fertile soil of intimate relationship with Jesus Christ.

We can never say, "Lord, we have nothing to feed them." If we know Jesus, we possess manna that will never run out, never dry up, and never grow stale. Feed his lambs with the food that God has given you: his love—stir fried or slow baked, marinated with the *essence* of his Spirit, served on a platter of humility, packed with powerful garnishes of your unique gifts. This is a meal fit for the King and for all future King's kids to enjoy.

Fast-food lunches fill temporary needs; they cannot provide lasting nourishment that feeds heart, soul, mind, and body. Only the Living Manna from Heaven can do that. It's the meal that will always satisfy.

### Personal Truth

*Too many unhealthy snacks can diminish our desire for the real Meal and leave our heavenly food supply depleted.*

### Personal Prayer

*Lord, I am so hungry for you and the sweet manna of your fellowship. May I never substitute empty calories for the life-giving manna you offer me daily.*

### Personal Question

*What kind of meals have you been serving lately?*

# OUR JUDGE AND ADVOCATE

*"Oh, that I had someone to hear me!*
*I sign now my defense—let the Almighty answer me."*

—Job 31:35

All Job wanted was his day in court. Like a prisoner accused of some horrid deed he did not commit, Job wanted to defend himself, to prove he was innocent. But also, he wanted to know this: why was he being punished when there was no crime? Was he being framed? Did God really think he had done something wrong?

This godly man endured untold suffering—the loss of almost everything he owned as well as his family and health. Then he suffered further as his friends tried to figure out his problem and made false assessments: "You must have sinned. Don't argue with authority. Just be quiet and take your punishment—or offer a plea bargain. Admit your crime, and maybe God will go easy on you."

Job was not claiming to be perfect. But he did know that his suffering was not the cause of any overt sin. Job just wanted to understand God more, what made God tick. "What kind of God would do this or allow this?" he wondered. "Maybe God is not in it at all."

From the onset, God declared his servant Job to be

"blameless and upright, a man who fears God and shuns evil" (Job 1:8). His response to Job ignored the issue of suffering, but he didn't really rebuke Job for his questions. Instead, God, in the tone of a righteous judge, offered a few questions of his own, revealing more of his mysterious power and awesome character in an even greater way:

> Each of us will stand in God's holy presence many times in our lives.

*Where were you when I laid the earth's foundation?*
*. . . Who marked off its dimensions?*
*Who stretched a measuring line across it?*
*. . . Who laid its cornerstone—*
*while the morning stars sang together*
*and all the angels shouted for joy?* (Job 38:4–7)

When God was finished, Job responded like a penitent, humbled child:

*Surely I spoke of things I didn't understand,*
*things too wonderful for me to know.*
*. . . My ears had heard of you*
*but now my eyes have seen you.*
*Therefore I despise myself*
*and repent in dust and ashes.* (Job 42:3, 5–6)

Inside all of us is a deep-down hunger to know this God personally. Perhaps we also long to go to another time and place where life is smoother and easier and God seems gentler and kinder—a time when things seem to make sense. We want a God we can figure out and don't need to question or understand. We like to put God in a box.

But God's ways are not our ways (Isaiah 55:8). Yet he wants us to know him, and he is willing to give each of us our day in court. In the same way that Job cried out to understand and be understood, and for the chance to argue his case before God the Judge, we, too, may cry out—especially in difficult times. When Jesus became our Advocate, that allowed us to come into the Judge's presence.

Each of us will stand in God's holy presence many times in our lives. As God allows us to enter his court, we will see the resurrected Savior who sits on the right hand of God as our Advocate. And God will listen to our questions as we honestly seek his answers about troubling issues.

When we finish, I imagine God's words, gentle but firm: "Where were you when my Son bled out his life for you? Did you die for the sins of the whole universe? Were you wise enough to devise a plan that would end all suffering forever after death?"

And in the presence of a holy, loving God who sent his own perfect Son to suffer death, we, like Job, will stand dumb. If we had truly understood who God was, perhaps we would not have waited until suffering or testing had ravaged our lives. We would have run to him sooner, for a different reason. We would have known his ways are beyond finding out, and that it was not even necessary to question them.

> God the Judge wants to gives us another glimpse of his multifaceted heart through our Advocate, Jesus Christ.

Our hearts would have cried out in searing pain, not because of our own puny suffering, but because we felt his.

God's words to us are designed to deepen our understanding of him. God the Judge wants to gives us another glimpse of his multifaceted heart through our Advocate, Jesus Christ.

If we know him personally, we may appear in "court" many other times as our enemy accuses us relentlessly. If seeds of sin in our lives have contributed to our suffering, God will show us those issues and draw us back into right fellowship with him (Psalm 139:23-24). And each time, our Advocate will turn to our Father Judge in the presence of our accuser, extend his nail-scarred hands, and say, "I declare this one to be innocent. My blood has paid the price."

Our final day in court will come as we stand before the Father "Judge" in heaven in eternity. That time, questions will truly seem unimportant. Joy will replace any pain and suffering we experienced on earth as we hear our Master's voice: "Well done, good and faithful servant!" (Matt. 25:21).

As long as we remain on this earth, our times with God the Judge will not eliminate all suffering; nor will they end all our questions. But they can open our hearts to a greater enjoyment and appreciation of who God really is when we realize that any day of the year, we can have our day in his court. We don't need to understand everything. We just need to know we are right with the Judge. As true children of God, we can "approach the throne of grace with confidence, so that we may receive mercy and find grace to help us in our time of need" (Heb. 4:16).

God may not give us the answers we want or ask for. But, just like Job, when we get a fresh glimpse of who God really is and view a snapshot of his heart, the questions lose their significance.

## PERSONAL TRUTH

*Sometimes, in the presence of God, silence may well be the best policy.*

## PERSONAL PRAYER

*God, thank you for being a just Judge, for hearing my questions, even when you may choose not to answer in this lifetime. Thank you for showing me more of yourself each time I come to you. And most of all, thank you for sending Jesus to be my Advocate.*

## PERSONAL QUESTION

*In your day in court, what questions would you like to ask God?*

# THE RESTORER OF YOUR SOUL

*Then Nathan said to David, "You are the man!"*

—2 Samuel 12:7

It was springtime, when kings went off to war. Only King David stayed home. That decision not to fight changed his life forever. Proud and powerful, David was struck with spring fever and a temptation—which he also chose not to fight.

Bored one night while his army was out defending his nation Israel for him, David strolled along the palace roof. His eyes fell on a beautiful woman bathing. By then, David was used to winning, and victory had snared his heart. He should have made a covenant similar to Job's: not to look at a woman with lust (31:1). Instead of turning his back, David took a second look. He lingered long enough to send someone to inquire about the identity of the woman.

No one likes saying no to the king, so David got what he wanted. Afterward, Bathsheba, the beautiful object of his lust, returned home after an evening affair with the king. Soon a problem developed: her pregnancy test turned up pink. Only David suddenly didn't feel in the pink. One sin led to another, and David ultimately committed not only adultery, but murder. Desperate, scared, and unrepentant, David issued the order to place Bathsheba's husband, Uriah, on the front line of battle, insuring his certain death.

After Uriah's death and Bathsheba's proper time of mourning, she married David and they lived happily ever after. Right? Not exactly.

The Bible says, "But GOD was not at all pleased with what David had done" (2 Samuel 12:1 MSG). So why didn't God take David out immediately and say to everyone, "I am a holy God! I will not be mocked. You disobey—you die!"

> But God seeks repentant hearts—those who, when confronted, will confess, "Yes, Lord, I am that man [or woman]."

God never breaks his promises, and the covenant he had made years earlier was still intact: God promised to build an everlasting kingdom through David's lineage (see 2 Samuel 23:5). This man after God's own heart had obvious weaknesses, but God wanted him back. The entire incident might have been swept under the carpet, because those who challenged kings did not live to talk about it. But God cared.

So he sent the prophet Nathan to confront David, which resulted in David's confession and repentance. David was indeed the man! Psalm 51 records David's heartrending cry of repentance to God. He was not sorry because he got caught, or just because he committed adultery and murder. In addition, David mourned because he realized he had sinned against God himself.

David did not escape the consequences of his sin. No one ever does. The son of David's illicit union died, his kingdom experienced confusion and turmoil, his enemies lost their respect for him, and later one of his own sons rebelled.

Yet God restored to David the joy of his salvation (Ps. 51:12). God hated the sin, but he loved David.

God truly knows the hearts of men and women and that all are prone to stray. But God seeks repentant hearts—those who, when confronted, will confess, "Yes, Lord, I am that man [or woman]." And what God wants to hear after those words is, "But I want to be your man [or woman] from this point on."

We are always at war with the one who wants to destroy us. Letting down our guard even once in boredom may plant seeds of sin. Unfortunately, those seeds sprout up like thorns that wound others, us, and ultimately, our God himself.

God will not abandon his warriors, but he will prune and shape them for the sake of his name, and because of his great love. He will accomplish his plans, because he is not willing for anything to destroy his purpose for our lives.

Regardless of where we are in life, God wants us to pick up our armor and rejoin the war for purity, for goodness, and for righteousness. We serve the King of kings. Even resting does not mean laying aside our defenses or armor. Refusing to wear the armor of God leaves our hearts, our minds, and our souls exposed. Only the "full armor of God" will enable us to resist (Eph. 6:11).

> God will not abandon his warriors, but he will prune and shape them for the sake of his name, and because of his great love.

A father who truly loves his child will never look the other way and allow his child to disobey without consequence. Neither will God. To do so would have meant destruction for David, and God had other plans for this chosen servant. God loved enough to confront, to shape, and to prune whatever was necessary to win back David's heart.

David said, "My sin is always before me" (Ps. 51:3). But David never forgot one thing he learned as a young shepherd in the desert. In the familiar Psalm 23 he wrote about the God he loved: "He restores my soul" (v. 2). Like a familiar shepherd's staff, God's grace and kindness and love would lead David daily. Only God could restore his soul.

When that happened, David knew sweet fellowship would again flood his life like a fountain. He knew that only in the presence of the Lord could real joy ever return.

### PERSONAL TRUTH

*Whatever we have done or will do can never erase God's love.*

### PERSONAL PRAYER

*Lord, thank you for grace, the kind of forgiveness that refuses to leave us alone or forsake us, even in our unworthiness. Cleanse us completely, and restore our hearts that we might return to you the love you so deserve.*

### PERSONAL QUESTION

*Have you ever experienced a time when God restored your soul?*

# ABBA, YOUR "DADDY"

*For you did not receive a spirit that makes you a slave*
*again to fear,*
*but you received the Spirit of sonship And by him we cry,*
*"Abba, Father."*

—Romans 8:15

The sweetest name a child can call an earthly father is *Daddy*. But in many formal cultures, *Daddy* was or is not always an allowable term. In earlier centuries, a father's name was spoken more as a title rather than a term of endearment, such as *Sir* or *Father*. Indeed, in early biblical times God himself was called by terms that reflected a more reverent and distant relationship.

Richard Foster says:

*To the faithful Jew who even hesitated to speak the Divine Name,*
*the childlike intimacy of Jesus' words [Abba, Father] must have*
*been utterly shocking.*

*Abba and imma—daddy and mommy—are the first words*
*Jewish children learn to speak. And abba is so personal, so*
*familiar a term that no one ever dared to use it in address to the*
*great God of the universe—no one until Jesus.*

*Professor Joachim Jeremias declares, "There is not a single example of the use of abba . . . as an address to God in the whole of Jewish literature."[24]*

If you accept Christ's offer of life and have become his child, then you have moved to a new level of relationship.

Yet over two thousand years ago, Jesus called God his "Abba, Father" (Mark 14:36). Paul used this affectionate term in the same breath as his reference to God and his Spirit.

This is the same God who had been known for centuries as Jehovah, as God Almighty, as the All-Powerful One—the one to be feared, reverenced, and respected. And he will always be that. It was God's fearful power that got Paul's attention in the first place. God blinded Paul temporarily while he was pursuing Christians and turned his heart and life around.

Then, years later in a Roman prison, Paul testified to a most enjoyable relationship with this same fearful God. Along with knowing a sovereign God, Paul had come to know a tender God who had sustained him, led him, and comforted him in every conceivable situation. Paul knew this God on a first-name basis, and he established a strong, intimate love relationship with him.

Paul had been an adamant, upright, legalistic Jew—one Christians feared. This same Paul said to his Christian friends: "Don't go back to the former days of formal laws that give no life! That's not what saved you! That spirit of fear—the fear that if you did not keep the law, you would perish—is not the spirit God has now given you. If you accept Christ's offer of life and have become his child, then you have moved to a new level of relationship. You now have received the spirit of sonship. God is not your taskmaster. He is your loving Father." Paul had come to understand the meaning of the joyful name *Abba*.

So did one orphan boy. A young couple went to an eastern country to adopt a child. They had waited and saved for years for that moment. In a nation where adoption had previously been forbidden, the laws had finally changed, the proper authority had been given, and they had completed all the necessary paperwork. The couple had prayed day and night for the child they would adopt and couldn't wait until they could claim a child as their own. Childless for years, they relished the idea of finally having a family.

They finally met the prospective child. They threw their arms open wide to receive him. But instead of running to their embrace, the young child, filled with terror, ran the opposite direction. Sobbing, he clutched a tattered, stuffed bear and buried his head in the pillow of the tiny cot that had been his "home"—all he had known.

The one in charge began to whisper into the boy's ear one more time exactly why the lovely couple had come. Almost an hour passed while the couple waited patiently in the next room. Finally, the supervisor coaxed the child to return and brought him face-to-face with the anxious couple. The father once again held out his arms, extending a fluffy, new teddy bear. Slowly and tenderly, the supervisor began to interpret the young father's wooing words as he spoke gently to the boy: "I will never hurt you. I will always love you. I want you to be our very own child. I paid a great price so I could make you part of our family. We have prepared a special room for you—one just your size where you can play and sleep and grow and be loved. From now on, I will

> Our heavenly Father comes to us and says: "I love you so much I sent my very own Son to claim you."

be your father. But I want you to call me 'Daddy,' because I will always love you, and I will always be your daddy."

The child's eyes lit up, and without hesitation he ran to his new father's arms, smiling and calling "Papa!" which was "Daddy" in his own language.

Our heavenly Father comes to us and says: "I love you so much I sent my very own Son to claim you. I have given him authority to issue you adoption papers. Before now, it was impossible to have a relationship with you. The laws of sin would not allow it. But now, my Son has paid a great price to adopt you into my family. I will never hurt you. I will always love you. You will never need to run away from me. I have created a special place for you in my heart. There, you can live and breathe and move around in great freedom and enjoyment—and you will be loved. I am now your Father. From now on, I want you to call me 'Abba' or 'Daddy.' I will be your daddy for eternity."

It doesn't get any better than that!

### PERSONAL TRUTH

*Family is a four-letter word spelled A-B-B-A.*

### PERSONAL PRAYER

*Father, what a delight to call you "Daddy"! I am so grateful you adopted me into your family. Why on earth would I ever want to run away from you?*

### PERSONAL QUESTION

*Which name do you use most when addressing God?*

# THE GOD WHO
# NEVER FORGETS

*Can a mother forget her little child and not have love for her
    own son?*
*Yet even if that should be, I will not forget you.*

—Isaiah 49:15 TLB

It happens so often, I have decided someone should engrave the words on my tombstone: "She forgot." Last week it was a phone number. The week before that, it was a major bill. This week, the checkbook is missing. And I can't remember where I saw it last. I am convinced someone is sneaking into my home and rearranging things so I will be purposely confused and rendered ineffective.

Then the phone rings. It is my daughter. And I remember: there are *some* things I hope I will never forget. I hope never to forget my daughters' names or how much I love them. I pray I will never forget the "bill" I owe God for giving us such beautiful, godly children. And since he paid the price and says I owe nothing but love and obedience, why do I need a checkbook anyway? I feel better already.

God seems to infer that our memories are not perfect, but a mom will not purposely forget about the baby she's nursing.

She remembers the pain of childbirth, but joy in the new birth soon replaces the difficult experience (John 16:21). Hebrew mothers often nursed their babies into the early years of their little lives. Can you imagine Jochebed forgetting about her infant son, Moses? Or Mary, the mother of Jesus? Or even aged Sarah, who finally bore a child at the age of ninety?

> Compassion is always in fashion for the mom who truly cares for her child.

Women are born with built-in kindness and mercy, are they not? Compassion is always in fashion for the mom who truly cares for her child. But wait a minute. The next line in Isaiah 49:15 says these words: "Yet even if that [forgetting] should be. . . . "

True. We may *want* to forget our children's names as raging hormones and peer pressures of adolescence usher them into Jekyll and Hyde personalities overnight. And during those years, we may lean more toward justice than compassion. But can a young mother truly forget about a young child so dependent upon her for every need? Apparently so, given the right conditions. The Hebrew word for "forget" here can also mean "to neglect," "to be unmindful," "to ignore," or "to overlook."

It happened just the other day. Another mom forgot about her toddler, who was buckled into the backseat of the van—in sweltering heat in the middle of summer. This child lived— barely. But others in the same situation have died. In most similar cases the social services translate "forgetting" as pure and simple *neglect*.

And even when a woman is young, her delicate brain wires may short-circuit. An accident may leave a mother with amnesia in the prime of her life. For any of us, senility may set in, along with conditions like dementia or Alzheimer's. People can and do forget, even the most intimate details—and people—in their lives.

It's not likely that a young mother will purposely neglect, overlook, or totally forget about her baby. But God, who created us, and who knows all hearts and minds, says, "Yet even if that [forgetting] should be. . . ." And then we read the rest of the story. God was using a comparison to prove a point.

Israel—despondent, crushed repeatedly, longing for hope and comfort from its promised Deliverer—wailed like a forlorn child buckled into a backseat of bondage, abandoned by its parent in the hot, sweltering desert: "The Lord has forsaken me; the Lord has forgotten me." They had heard the promise, but they had seen no deliverance. They were gasping for a breath of fresh, cool air, dying for relief. So God gave it—the reminder that God had made clear since his promise to Abraham: "I will not forget you!" The same God who "does not slumber or sleep" (Psalm 121:3) never forgets about us. And then, as if to give them one final proof, God added this statement: "See, I have engraved you on the palms of my hands" (Isa. 49:16).

That sentence sends chills up my spine. God, Israel's Deliverer, gave them a glimpse of a future that would ultimately fulfill his covenant to everyone, for all time. It was not just a promise to the Jewish people. He enlarged it for the whole world.

> The same God who "does not slumber or sleep" (Psalm 121:3) never forgets about us.

Centuries later, a follower named Thomas needed to hear that same message. The disciples had watched their beloved Jesus die. They saw the Christ, the Son of God, the fulfillment of every prophecy, the long-awaited Messiah, hanging on a cross with spikes driven into his hands and feet. Jesus was gone. Although many of the disciples had seen him resurrected, Thomas had not. Everything within Thomas cried out, "He has forgotten me!" So he said, "Unless I see the nail marks in his hands and put my finger where the nails were, and put my hand into his side, I will not believe it" (John 20:25).

A week later, Jesus showed up. And before Thomas could even say a word, Jesus turned his hands palms up and addressed Thomas. "Put your finger here; see my hands. . . . Stop doubting and believe" (John 20:27).

Even today, we have never felt so alone. Darkness has overtaken us, and there is no one around who cares. We feel like the whole world has caved in, and we have nowhere to turn. Our source of despair may be a broken marriage, or the loss of a child. Maybe a job termination. Perhaps a call from the surgeon or police station. In our helpless state, all we can do is cry out, "God, have you forgotten me?"

And in the same way that the Father and Son did for Israel and for Thomas and the disciples, Jesus comes to us with palms turned upward and speaks to us ever so gently but firmly: "Though others may forget, I will never forget you. See, here's the proof. Within these scars, your name is engraved on my heart forever. I did this for you! Now stop doubting and believe."

He is the God Who Never Forgets. When you know him personally, he will allow you a glimpse of his nail-scarred hands. Imagine your joyful surprise when you see your own name engraved on the palm of that hand, written in red!

## PERSONAL TRUTH

*Never forget to thank God that he remembers you.*

## PERSONAL PRAYER

*Lord, physical circumstances may steal my memory, but may I never forget to thank you for your precious love. I have engraved your words in my heart, Lord. Thank you that you never forget me!*

## PERSONAL QUESTION

*Have you ever felt like God has forgotten you?*

# THE GOD WHO
# DELIGHTS IN YOU

*For the LORD takes delight in his people;*
*he crowns the humble with salvation.*

—Psalm 149:4

They had met in college. But Sam now worked on the East Coast, and Judy lived on the West. Both found fulfilling careers that prevented them from seeing one another very often. They talked by phone or E-mail once a week, but even those times seemed scarce.

Furthermore, they soon discovered some barriers. Sam was married to his work. Judy enjoyed ocean retreats. Sam lived on take-out nutrition. Judy loved gourmet cooking. Sam saw no need for religion. Judy embraced them all. For several years they tried to maintain a relationship in the hopes that they could be married someday, when their schedules changed. But neither wanted to give or adjust, and their interest soon waned. Before long, Judy made the first confession: "I just can't find enjoyment in a long-distance relationship. I need more than that." They parted painfully.

Long-distance relationships rarely grow at the same pace as

others. And it's hard to get to know someone, much less enjoy him or her, if you never spend time together.

The psalmist David knew that. "Delight yourself in the LORD," he said, "and he will give you the desires of your heart" (Ps. 37:4). He repeatedly expressed his pleasure in the Lord and encouraged others to "magnify," "praise," "sing praises to," "bless," "give thanks to," "and rejoice" in the Lord. God was more to him than someone in the distant heavens. David knew how to enjoy God!

> And with the fierce passion that only love can bring, Jesus showed us that love as he died for us.

David understood relationships take time. And in the fields watching sheep, composing songs for the Lord, hiding in caves from his enemies, dancing after a great victory, and even following times of great failure and repentance, David knew how to find joy in his God. He celebrated God's creation, meditated on his lessons, gave glory to God in battle, poured out his heart when discouraged and afraid, and ran to him for mercy and grace. He was anything but perfect. But David loved and enjoyed God. No wonder God gave him the title "a man after my own heart" (Acts 13:22).

What about God? What about this holy, omniscient God who lives in the distant heavens? We are earthy, and God is heavenly. We are imperfect and God is perfect. We love sin. God loves holiness. We fail repeatedly. God never does. We are foolish. God is wise. Everyone knows that a long-distance relationship involving extremely different partners rarely makes a marriage.

But God is different. First, he *wants* a relationship with us. Second, he built a bridge from heaven to earth and made it possible to have one through his Son, Jesus Christ. And with the fierce passion that only love can bring, Jesus showed us that love as he died for us.

Maybe you're still wondering how God feels about you—*you* personally. Not just about the world, but you there, with the five preschool children. You, the computer addict, searching for the perfect relationship. What about you there, sleeping under the city's bridge? Yes, you, working two jobs trying to make ends meet, and you, who just lost your best friend. What about you, corporate president, schoolteacher, waitress, or college student?

The psalmist's words were written for you—and me: "The LORD takes delight in his people." God not only loves you, he takes delight in you! Have you ever met a new parent or grandparent without at least one brag book to share? They take delight in their children! The Hebrew words for "take delight in" may also carry the connotation of "finding pleasure," "accepting," "being pleased with," "approves," "holds in high esteem," and yes, even "enjoys." We make God happy! God enjoys us! And he wants us to enjoy him. Our names are even written in his brag book!

He not only delights in us while we live here on earth, but one day he is planning a grand celebration for those who know and love him. Using yet another Hebrew word for "delight," the Bible says, "He will take great delight in you, / he will quiet you with his love, / he will rejoice over you with singing" (Zeph. 3:17). The idea here is that God will take great pleasure in celebrating us in heaven. God never stops enjoying the ones he loves!

> God never stops enjoying the ones he loves!

Rick Warren says, "If you are *that* important to God, and he considers you valuable enough to keep you with him for eternity, what greater significance could you have? You are a child of God, and you bring pleasure to God like nothing else he has ever created."[25]

God longs for you to know that he chose you for his pleasure and purpose (Eph. 1:5). If you have not crossed the bridge he provided for beginning an intimate relationship with him, what's stopping you?

Once you come to know joyfully and intimately the God Who Delights in You, you'll never settle for a long-distance acquaintance again.

### PERSONAL TRUTH

*People don't fall in love; they grow in love.*

### PERSONAL PRAYER

*Lord, just to know that my life brings joy to you and that you delight in me makes me want to run to your arms even more—and to bring pleasure to your heart any way I can.*

### PERSONAL QUESTION

*When do you most enjoy God?*

# THE PERFECT GUEST

*"Zacchaeus, come down immediately.*
*I must stay at your house today."*
*So he came down at once and welcomed him gladly.*

—Luke 19:5–6

I was skeptical, but the caller on the other end of the phone insisted. "I'd like to come out to your house and interview you."

As a young teacher in a Vacation Bible school class in our church that summer, I had taught the older children a unique way to combat temptation in their lives. We all made Anti-Satan Kits, a concept originating with author C. S. Lovett. Each child chose Bible verses that dealt with a particular temptation they might face, such as lying, cheating, expressing anger, or disobeying parents. On one side of an index card they listed the temptation, and on the opposite side a Scripture to help give them strength to fight it. Since the Bible teaches that when we hide God's Word in our hearts, it will help us not to disobey, we knew the importance of memorizing Scripture and making it a part of our lives (see Ps. 119:11).

I also wrote a newspaper column for my town at that time. A larger metroplex newspaper picked up on my column one week, in which I had told about that particular Vacation Bible school project. The reporter who called wanted to know more about this Anti-Satan Kit. I'm sure it sounded, well, intriguing to him.

When the reporter arrived, he immediately began looking around at the walls and firing questions. "Tell me more about the class you taught. Where is your Anti-Satan Kit? May I see it?"

> "Christ is the head of this house, the unseen guest at every meal, the silent listener to every conversation."

I wondered later if he expected to see a box of mystical powder or a magic wand, because he seemed disappointed when I pulled out a simple stack of index cards enclosed in a small, plastic sleeve. All the time, he kept moving through the rooms of my home, his eyes scanning the walls as if searching for something else. Finally, he stopped abruptly in the hallway, staring at a plaque on the wall. Then he blurted, "Don't you have any other religious things on the wall?"

I realized then what the reporter had been hunting for. "No," I replied softly, not intending any sarcasm or disrespect. "Jesus is in my heart, not on my walls."

Once again he looked disappointed, but he asked me to stand beside a crooked plaster-of-Paris wall plaque someone had given us years before. We had little money at the time to invest in expensive wall décor of any kind. The words on the plaque read: "Christ is the head of this house, the unseen guest at every meal, the silent listener to every conversation."

The reporter sighed, snapped my picture, and made a hasty exit. The next week, my picture appeared on the religious page of the newspaper. There I was, standing beside that crooked picture.

The Bible tells us that an "unseen guest" made an appearance in Jericho one day to visit a man's home. And he, too, did not go by direct invitation. The visitor obviously came looking for something—or someone.

Jesus was just passing through Jericho one day when he stopped, looked up at the sky, and saw a curious sight. There, two beady eyes peered down at him from the shady branches of a huge sycamore-fig tree. Like a curious child, because of the surrounding crowds, the little man had climbed the tree to get a better view of Jesus.

Jesus' voice must have startled the man, especially when he heard the stranger call his name. "Zacchaeus, come down immediately. I must stay at your house today."

Biblical customs included providing hospitality for strangers, and Zacchaeus felt honored to have the privilege. Few people ever wanted to be seen or associated with Zacchaeus, much less sit under his roof, eat his meals, or *stay* there for any length of time. Needless to say, Zacchaeus had few friends. He was a tax collector, the dreaded enemy of the common, hardworking Jew.

Zacchaeus responded to Jesus with joy and welcomed him. But other people observing Jesus responded in disgust. Zacchaeus's stature matched their views of him: they thought *little* of him. They criticized Jesus for even wanting to be a guest of a "sinner."

In Zacchaeus's home, we become the unseen guests as well as the silent listeners. The Bible does not let us eavesdrop on all that transpired that day. One thing we can probably guess: whatever Jesus said or did, he probably didn't examine the walls of Zaccheus's home looking for religious evidence. Instead, he looked straight into the tax collector's heart. What he saw there was a picture of a crooked man, steeped in dishonesty. Under the penetrating gaze of

> When he finds a home for *his* heart, he is no longer an unseen guest.

Jesus, no one can remain unchanged. No magic powder, no hocus-pocus, just one look.

And instead of gathering proof with which to disprove Zacchaeus' credibility, Jesus reached into the man's heart and hung a new plaque. Zaccheus stood up, and the fruit of a changed heart emerged. Instead of offering what might be required or expected as restoration from thieves, the crooked tax collector turned into a generous banker. He was so moved by Jesus' visit to his home that his joy overflowed. He offered to give half of his possessions to the poor and to pay back four times the amount of what he had cheated anyone in taxes.

The visit ended, but not before Jesus made clear his mission. Apparently Jesus had come searching for something—and found it. "You are the reason I have come: to seek and to save what was lost" (see Luke 19:10).

Jesus, the Perfect Guest, does not force his way into anyone's heart, but he does come to each of us, seeking a place to stay. And when he finds a home for *his* heart, he is no longer an unseen guest. He is then the true Head of the house. We are now part of his family.

And we are both overjoyed at the new relationship.

## PERSONAL TRUTH

*Jesus loves to make himself at home in our hearts.*

## PERSONAL PRAYER

*Lord, thank you for the privilege of being in your family. You are the head of my home, and the head of my heart. May you always feel welcome here.*

## PERSONAL QUESTION

*Is Jesus a guest or a permanent resident of your home?*

DAY 31

# THE GOD OF ALL AGES

*He did what was right in the eyes of the LORD*
*and walked in the ways of his father David,*
*not turning aside to the right or to the left.*

—2 Chronicles 34:2

Most people attribute wisdom to those with gray hair and senior citizens—which, by the way, qualifies the majority of baby boomers. After all, isn't wisdom something that only age can bring? But maturity—and godliness—is not always measured in years. At least not in the case of Josiah.

At age eight, Josiah was one of the youngest kings ever to reign. The Bible praises him with this astounding statement about his kingdom and the people he ruled: "As long as he lived, they did not fail to follow the LORD, the God of their fathers" (2 Chron. 34:33). How did that happen? He must have had a godly father or grandfather who walked the walk and talked the talk.

But if you look back a chapter or two, regarding Josiah's grandfather you will discover this statement: "He did evil in the sight of the LORD, following the detestable practices of the nations the LORD had driven out before the Israelites." The record further adds, "Manasseh also shed so much innocent blood that he filled Jerusalem from end to end" (2 Chron. 33:2;

2 Kings 21:16). Part of that blood belonged to his own sons, whom he sacrificed on the altar of a heathen god.

So much for Josiah's grandfather's potentially good influence. Manasseh did have a change of heart, however, when the

> The truth is God holds each of us responsible for our own attitudes, thoughts, and actions.

nation of Assyria put a hook in his nose and shackles on his feet. He learned his lesson, and God restored this broken, humbled king. Manasseh set to work trying to reverse his destruction, and the people returned to worshiping the Lord, although they used the pagan altars to make sacrifices to him. But how much more good he could have done— and how many lives could have been spared, if only he had listened to the Lord—and to his father—early on?

And as for Josiah's dad, Amon: he also started young, at the age of twenty-two. But he followed in his father's evil footsteps, and "unlike his father Manasseh, he did not humble himself before the LORD" (2 Chron. 33:23).

Perhaps Josiah was simply a puppet king and happened to have a godly crew of counselors in his cabinet, advising him day and night. They pulled the strings; he said yes. A great way to save face, fake wisdom, and live longer—and maybe gain God's favor in the meantime. But that doesn't appear to be the case, either.

The truth is God holds each of us responsible for our own attitudes, thoughts, and actions. He is a personal God who deals individually with his creations. I will not be judged by my father or grandfather's examples, be they good or bad, though I may be strongly influenced by their actions or teaching. God holds me accountable only for the choices I make.

Josiah made some wise choices. At only age sixteen, he "began to seek the God of his father David." Four years later he began a sweeping purge of ungodly influences in Judah and

Jerusalem, crushing idols and altars throughout Israel. Josiah meant business. Six more years passed, and he sent messengers to start repairing the temple "of the LORD his God" (2 Chron. 34:3, 8). When did Josiah make the Lord his God?

In the restoration process, Hilkiah the priest made a remarkable discovery. He unearthed a long-lost, dust-covered copy of the Book of the Law, which contained the same instructions written by the fiery fingers of God to Moses and his people. We can only speculate how Josiah found the courage to honor his God without instructions—and without the wise teachings of a godly father. Perhaps his mom read him Bible stories before he even learned to walk. Maybe she reminded him to follow the ways of his grandfather's last days, when with graying hair and as a senior, he finally sought God's wisdom.

Scribes of the Law carefully preserved the words of God through the years and passed them down from generation to generation. They were never lost entirely. And people still recognized and feared the true Jehovah God when they heard about him. Interestingly enough, the Bible linked Josiah's faith not to his own father, but to his "father" David. Our godly influence continues for generations. In fact twelve generations had passed since Josiah came on the scene after David.

> He is not a God who condemns us for our ancestors' failure without giving us a chance to repent.

When Josiah's secretary read to him from the Book of the Law, Josiah definitely recognized the book as God's Word; he immediately tore his robes as a sign of great distress, grief, and repentance. He was glad to uncover the book but mournful that his people had left their first love. He instructed the priest to go find someone who could help him appeal to a God who must be angry at his nation's prior disobedience.

The words that returned were those of a God who is compassionate. He is not a God who condemns us for our ancestors' failure without giving us a chance to repent. There is such a thing as corporate discipline and punishment, and God determines a nation's fate in his own way and in his own time. And we may suffer along with others. But he is also a God who responds to our personal obedience (Josh. 1:7).

In Josiah's case, God did not abort his plans to discipline the nation that had turned against him. But he did give them a reprieve because of Josiah's humility before God. Josiah renewed his nation's covenant to God, and he enjoyed a peaceful and joyful relationship with God. Josiah, God promised, would not have to see the inevitable disaster and judgment of his hand.

In reality, wisdom—and joyful relationship—have nothing to do with age. Instead, wisdom has everything to do with God. Whether we come to God in our youth, our prime, or at the end of our lives, God will still deal with us individually.

This personal God is not only the God of the Ages. He is the God of *All* Ages.

## PERSONAL TRUTH

*The wise in heart have a heart for God.*

## PERSONAL PRAYER

*God, no matter what decisions I face, I cannot make them alone. Please grant me your wisdom. For all of my life, through all of my ages, I want to obey you with all of my heart.*

## PERSONAL QUESTION

*Are you influencing anyone positively today?*

# THE GOD OF INTERRUPTIONS

*When she heard about Jesus, she came up behind him in the*
   *crowd*
*and touched his cloak, because she thought,*
*"If I just touch his clothes, I will be healed."*

—Mark 5:27–28

S weat trickled down the backs of Jesus and his disciples. The crowd pressed close as the people pushed
and shoved to get a better look at the Savior, the wonder
worker. A man named Jairus, a synagogue ruler and father of
a twelve-year-old girl, dropped at Jesus' feet, begging him to
come and heal his dying daughter.

The man was frantic. He knew his daughter's life was hanging in the balance. Why wouldn't the people step aside and
allow Jesus to get to his house? Even minutes could mean the
difference between life and death. Jesus inched his way
through the crowd, but the pressing only increased.

Suddenly Jesus stopped in the middle of the road. The father frowned, wringing his hands and looking at the crowd as
if searching for someone—anyone—to urge the people out of
the way. All he could think of was his daughter's life. He remembered first holding her as a tiny infant, and the joy that
filled his heart as he looked into her eyes. He watched her take

her first steps as she toddled out to embrace him one day, and he could still smell the first honey cake she baked proudly for him. Her mother had taught her well in the ways of a woman.

Where had the years flown? Before long, she might even be promised to one of the Jewish young men in their synagogue. A man was proud to have his own son. But it would also bring him pleasure for his daughter to marry a godly man who might become a synagogue leader himself—and a son to him in his old age.

> But to Jesus, life had no real interruptions.

But if Jesus didn't hurry, his daughter would have no husband. And he would have no future son-in-law. He would have nothing but sorrow—and a daughter dead before her time.

Then Jesus spoke gently but firmly. "Who touched me?"

The disciples looked at one another in disbelief. "Not me," each said. They reminded Jesus that the crowd was like a sea around them. There were probably many who bumped into Jesus. It couldn't be helped.

But Jesus' words contained a greater meaning: "Someone touched me; I know that power has gone out from me." Not only did someone *touch* Jesus, that person touched his power intentionally. And Jesus knew it instantly.

Finally, a woman fell at Jesus' feet. For twelve years she had suffered from hemorrhaging. No doctors had helped. She was not only poor, but a social outcast who could never be considered "clean" and whole. And her condition had only worsened.

But touching the Master had brought the desired results. Something had happened to her, so she admitted the truth.

Jesus honored the faith of the woman and granted total healing. She could then return "in peace," freed from her emotional, physical, and spiritual suffering (Mark 5:34).

But the distraught father had not found freedom. His emotions were still tied in knots. Then a messenger arrived, announcing it was too late. His daughter was dead. The woman's interruption had cost Jairus his daughter's life. "Why bother the teacher any more?" cried the messenger above the alarming wails of the crowd (Mark 5:35).

But to Jesus, life had no real interruptions. Not really. Oh, there were things that seemed like interruptions. Each time Jesus attempted to rest from the crowd's press and cross to the other side of the lake, more people greeted him, crying out for help. The demon-possessed cursed at his name; the lame and the sick begged for mercy. Seekers wanted to know more; enemies tried to curtail his mission. Crises and needs followed Jesus like lambs seeking their mother's milk.

But interruptions? Not to Jesus. Interruptions represented people. And people were his business. People were his purpose. Interruptions spelled opportunities to display his Father's great power and love.

And in the grander scheme of things, interruptions never slowed Jesus down or aborted his purpose. Which would represent the greater miracle to the father and his family: healing the girl's sickness or raising her from the dead? "The child is not dead but asleep," Jesus said to the crowd of mourners at the man's home (Mark 5:39). They erupted in laughter. But Jesus simply continued the work he had come to do, restoring the lost, healing the sick, glorifying his Father in whatever means that interruption afforded. And the girl lived again.

> Interruptions spelled opportunities to display his Father's great power and love.

One can only wonder at Jesus' deeper meaning. Even death is only an interruption, not the end of life as we know it.

I had one of "those" days recently. Three times the phone rang while I was working on a project I hoped would ultimately glorify my Father in heaven. Three times I hung up, a little too impatiently, ending the solicitor's spiel. And then the phone rang a fourth time. I stared at it as if it were an unwelcome intruder. After all, I was doing God's work—important stuff.

But God whispered to my heart, and I heard a gentle, "Not this time. Pick it up."

I started to object, but by the third ring, I surrendered. I listened as patiently as I could, then politely tried to convince the caller that I was satisfied with my product. I simply wasn't interested. And then I heard myself adding something totally off the wall: "But may I tell you something I am interested in?"

I shared my love for Jesus and what a wonder it was to know him and to write about him. Before I had finished, the caller was asking for prayer, and I learned the grander meaning of the word *interruption*.

Most of us would rather "let sleeping interruptions lie." We don't need them, and we don't want them. They represent not opportunities, but obstacles to our ultimate goals. But the sooner we learn to enjoy interruptions for what they are—personally designed encounters from God to make his ways known—the more we will learn to enjoy this wonderful, creative God of Interruptions.

### Personal Truth

*How we spend our time determines what we enjoy the most.*

### Personal Prayer

*Lord, turn every interruption into an opportunity to share your love. Forgive me for sometimes confusing my priorities. Enjoying you means enjoying every day as a gift from you.*

## PERSONAL QUESTION

*How do you handle interruptions?*

# THE GOD WHO SEES
# OUR POTENTIAL

*The LORD is with you, mighty warrior.*
—Judges 6:12

I t happens all the time: impersonal, corporate philosophy that says, "Fire the plodder. Hire the aggressive. Demote the weak and timid. Promote the strong and gifted." Seniority no longer demands respect. The next in line could be the last in line. Produce, produce, produce is the name of the game. And appearance makes all the difference. How else can a company survive?

Sounds reasonable. But a man named Gideon discovered that's not the way God does business. This fearful man was hiding out in a winepress threshing wheat when he suddenly found himself in what could be a scene on the set of *Touched by an Angel*. The angel of God was paying him a visit—and a strong compliment: "The LORD is with you, mighty warrior."

Gideon was sure heaven had assigned the angel a wrong address. He seemed to ignore the angel's compliment and instead took an opportunity to release some fairly hostile emotions. "If the LORD is with us, why has all this happened to us? Where are all his wonders that our fathers told us about

when they said, 'Did not the LORD bring us up out of Egypt?'
But the LORD has abandoned us and put us into the hand of
Midian" (Judg. 6:13).

Remember that Gideon was in the winepress—threshing
wheat. Not the usual place for this kind of
work. He and the other Israelites had
watched the Midianite raiders ransack their
land "like a swarm of locusts" (Judg. 6:5).
Every time the Israelites planted crops, their
enemies swooped in for the harvest. Like
squatters, the Midianites camped on the land
and destroyed even their livestock. So the
people had cried out to the Lord for help. Is
it any wonder that Gideon stared in disbelief
at the angel's words, "The LORD is with
you"?

> The Lord intended to use Gideon despite his weaknesses. In fact, it almost appears that God was choosing Gideon *because* of his weaknesses.

It was the angel's turn to ignore Gideon's words. Instead,
he handed Gideon his promotion papers another way. This
time Scripture records these not as words from the angel, but
from the Lord himself: "You are the one God will use to save
Israel. Go in the strength you have. I am sending you."

Gideon already knew he was anything but a "mighty warrior." Mighty warriors didn't hide from their enemies. His ex-
cuses were ready. "Who, me? My family is at the bottom of the
list of 'Who's Who.' And I am the puniest member of my family!" In other words, "What strength?" Even on the eve of battle, this timid leader still needed three tangible evidences to
assure him that God really would deliver his people through
Gideon.

The Lord intended to use Gideon despite his weaknesses.
In fact, it almost appears that God was choosing Gideon *because* of his weaknesses. Why else would God reduce his army

of thirty-two thousand to a puny band of three hundred to fight the gigantic Midianite army? Why else would he use trumpets, torches, and clay jars to frighten an enemy army into self-destruction?

Gideon was not the first person, nor the last, in which God delighted to turn a loser into a winner. Moses couldn't speak well; Jeremiah was too young; David was a runt; Peter, a coward. Saul was a murderer; Esther, a Jew. Not one, according to normal standards of his or her culture, would have been voted the Most Likely to Succeed. Yet God saw potential in them—and used them for his purpose.

The apostle Paul gave us a clue why God's qualifications for greatness include such unlikely candidates: "But God chose the foolish things of the world to shame the wise; God chose the weak things of the world to shame the strong. He chose the lowly things of this world and the despised things—and the things that are not—to nullify the things that are, so that no one may boast before him" (1 Cor. 1:27–29).

God saw the potential in a loser named Abraham Lincoln, who in his brief tenure as president effected more change and brought more freedom into our country than those who have served in government for five decades. God empowered a cerebral palsy victim named David Ring to dedicate his life to ministry, traveling around the world testifying to God's grace. And he chose a white-collar prisoner named Charles Colson to bring spiritual freedom into the lives of thousands of men and women locked behind bars.

> God also sees something inside that others cannot.

Why? Because God knows us inside and out. He knows our tendency to push the envelope when it comes time to promote ourselves and take credit for anything good. But God also sees something inside that others cannot. It's not that God is always rooting for the underdog; he uses men and women of strong, godly character. He delights in promoting those whose hearts are tender toward his, regardless of their status.

God looks into the heart, not at the outer appearance (1 Sam. 16:7). He knows that those who have nothing to offer but broken lives and hopeless futures—the recipients of the world's pink slips—have nowhere to go but up.

He sees the potential and delights in showing his light through the broken cracks of "clay pots"—those who are totally dependent on him. He knows these are the ones who will honor him the most, because he and those watching know there's no possible explanation for their employee success other than God.

Now that's the kind of employer I enjoy working for.

## PERSONAL TRUTH

*It's not what you do, but whom you serve, that determines your success.*

## PERSONAL PRAYER

*Lord, surely I must qualify as one of those clay pots. There is nothing of value in me but what you see. And there is nothing good that can come from this life, except what you produce. Thank you for visualizing potential in me. I will honor you with every success.*

## PERSONAL QUESTION

*How has God brought success out of your weakness?*

# THE VINE

*I am the Vine; you are the branches. . . .*
*I've told you these things for a purpose:*
*that my joy might be your joy, and your joy wholly mature.*
*This is my command: Love one another the way I loved you.*

—John 15:5, 11–12 MSG

Novelist Anna Quindlen offers some profound "soul" advice first written for college graduates:

*People don't talk about the soul very much anymore. It's so much easier to write a résumé than to craft a spirit. But a résumé is cold comfort on a winter night, or when you're sad, or broke, or lonely, or when you've gotten back the chest X-ray and it doesn't look so good. . . . Get a life in which you are not alone. . . . And remember that love is not leisure; it is work. Each time I look at my diploma, I remember that I am still a student, still learning everyday how to be human. . . . Consider the lilies of the field. Look at the fuzz on a baby's ear. . . . The classroom is everywhere. The exam comes at the very end.*[26]

In another place, and a much earlier time, another "graduation" ceremony took place. Story time was over. The Teacher had done his job. His assignment was almost finished. But first, Jesus summarized the material and offered some final instructions.

For three years Jesus had poured his life into his disciples—his chosen "dirty dozen" who had followed him day and night. They'd witnessed miracles, they'd escaped death, they'd tasted victory. And everywhere they'd walked with Jesus, they'd felt the touch of heaven.

> As long as the branches were attached to the Vine, they would bear fruit.

But then Jesus gathered his beloved men into the Upper Room, where they would share a final meal. Jesus had more to offer. What he really wanted to give them was some "soul" food.

Once the betraying disciple, Judas Iscariot, had left, Jesus began telling his disciples about a new command: "Love one another. In the same way I loved you, you love one another. This is how everyone will recognize that you are my disciples—when they see the love you have for each other" (John 13:34–35 MSG).

But the disciples interrupted him by wanting to know where he planned to go—and why they could not go with him. They still didn't get it. Jesus was going to die. And when he did, it would be extremely important that they remembered and fulfilled his new command. Seeing their need for comfort and explanation, Jesus answered their questions as plainly as he could. He would not leave them alone. The Comforter, the Holy Spirit—his presence in every believer—would come. But only if he left. Jesus was thinking of them. But they were thinking only of themselves. Grief often does that to us for a season.

They left that place, but Jesus continued teaching. Then he compared himself to a vine, and his disciples were the branches. As long as the branches were attached to the Vine, they would bear fruit. If cut off, they would end up as deadwood. "I've loved you the way my Father has loved me," Jesus added. "Make yourselves at home in my love." And then Jesus repeated the new command, "Love one another" (John 15:9, 12 MSG).

Why had he spent three years teaching and demonstrating love to them? Because he knew it was the secret to joy. Unless they stayed connected to the Vine, they could not love. And if they did not love, they would "graduate" with no joy. It was not a joy of their making. It was the joy of Jesus himself.

As a mother experiences agony during childbirth, the disciples would experience the pain and grief of Jesus' death. But Jesus knew that after his resurrection and the coming of the Holy Spirit, his disciples would be empowered to love like never before. What would replace that grief? His joy. The joy of obedience—of loving others and following him.

Jesus was not asking them to revert to a faith built on keeping the Law. A diploma from the School of Law Keeping is, as Anna Quindlen said, "cold comfort on a winter night, or when you're sad, or broke, or lonely, or when you've gotten back the chest X-ray and it doesn't look so good." And a diploma from the School of Law Keeping will count for nothing when the final test is given at the end of our lives.

> Only one who was attached to the true Vine could understand the origin of that joy.

Laws simply point out our need. But Jesus' *new* commandment of love goes beyond the school of law. It meets our deepest needs. Jesus' new commandment involves, once again, the principle of continual relationship. Jesus wants all people to enjoy the same kind of love connection he has experienced with his Father.

Paul spoke about this love years later when as an imprisoned follower of Christ, he pointed out the relationship of the

Vine to its branches. The result of that unbroken connection is fruit. The fruit of the Spirit—God's Spirit actively at work in us—is love, joy, peace. . . . Only one who was attached to the true Vine could understand the origin of that joy.

Jesus' graduation address to his disciples ended. But for them, it was only the beginning. He did not just leave them with temporary joy—the memories of three wonderful years attending the School of Jesus. He then offered them an honorary doctorate degree of complete joy—joy that was perfect, mature, and rooted in him. Because Jesus loved them, they could love each other. Because they loved each other, others could see Jesus. When others see Jesus, they experience joy. When others experience joy, they love too. It is not something they will do in between jobs, children, or Monday night football. Love involves work. But even the work itself—of staying connected to the Vine—is a joy.

And in time, the disciples, and we with them, come to understand that in God's school of loving, class is never out. His Spirit is always teaching, always giving, always loving. And even for the ones who hated school, that truth brings great comfort and joy.

### PERSONAL TRUTH

*God is the only one who can turn grief to real joy.*

### PERSONAL PRAYER

*Lord, thank you for your Spirit and the comfort he brings daily. I am willing to attend school the rest of my life, if it means you will be my Teacher.*

### PERSONAL QUESTION

*How is your "joy gauge" reading lately?*

# THE GOD WHO LIVES
# AMONG US

*What the king asks is too difficult.*
*No one can reveal it to the king except the gods,*
*and they do not live among men.*

—Daniel 2:11

It's no picnic to fall into the hands of an angry ruler. It could even cost you your life. Just ask Daniel and his three friends.

Daniel, Hananiah, Mishael, and Azariah were sons of Jewish royalty taken captive during the siege of Jerusalem. King Nebuchadnezzar assigned them foreign names: Beltashazar, Shadrach, Meshach, and Abednego. He arranged for them to receive the best instruction available in Babylonian literature and culture. Most young men of their age, after being thoroughly brainwashed for three years in the occult, sorcery, and pagan religions, would emerge completely confused and cleansed of any former connection to the God they once proclaimed.

But these men were different. From the get-go Daniel, their spokesman, resolved to live without defiling himself—beginning with the king's mandated rich, royal foods. After ten days, their diet of vegetables and water made them healthier than any others, so they earned the privilege of continuing to choose their own meals.

God honored and blessed these four young men of strong character, and they excelled in all kinds of knowledge and understanding. To Daniel, God gave a special gift: to interpret dreams and visions of all kinds.

> Shadrach, Meshach, and Abednego stood on the truth that their God would rescue them.

That came in handy when the king happened to be a heavy dreamer. In the second year of King Nebuchadnezzar's reign, he had troubled dreams no one could understand. When pressed to interpret, his own best astrologers said, "No one can do that! Only gods—and they don't live among us!" They were right. But they didn't know Daniel's God.

Daniel intervened and partially agreed with the astrologers: "No wise man, enchanter, magician or diviner can explain to the king the mystery he has asked about, but there is a God in heaven who reveals mysteries" (Dan. 2:27–28). So Daniel interpreted the dream according to God's instructions. And the king promoted Daniel.

Perhaps even Daniel and his three friends still had much to learn about this God in heaven. When the king declared that the whole province in Babylonia must bow down to a newly built golden statue where Shadrach, Meshach, and Abednego lived, Daniel's three friends refused. This, despite the decree: "Whoever does not fall down and worship will immediately be thrown into a blazing furnace" (Dan. 3:6). (Daniel, who remained at the royal court, is not mentioned here with his friends, and we are not told why.)

The Bible says faith, when tested by fire, emerges pure as

gold (see 1 Pet. 1:7). Shadrach, Meshach, and Abednego stood on the truth that their God would rescue them. "But if not," they added, "we still will not deny our faith" (see Dan. 3:18).

King Nebuchadnezzar was so incensed, he fired up the flames seven times hotter. The fire was so hot, several of his soldiers were sucked into the flames and instantly consumed.

But it is a far more fearful thing to fall into the hands of an angry God. King Nebuchadnezzar was watching and suddenly discovered the secret of this God who interpreted dreams, saved some people, and consumed others. The God of Daniel, Shadrach, Meshach, and Abednego was not just a mortal god whose altars could be destroyed with one blow. He was not just a God in heaven who is wise and all-discerning. There were not three men in the fire. The king counted four. And Shadrach, Meshach, and Abednego walked out of the fire shining like gold.

Perhaps the king remembered the words of the astrologers: "No one [can do that] except the gods, and they do not live among men."

But this God does. He lives and breathes and walks among us daily—in the home where some of our greatest testing comes, in the workplace, when we are often cast into the flames of controversy, or even on the battlefield, where terrorists wait to consume us with the fires of their hatred. Wherever we go, he is there.

> **Wherever we go, he is there.**

Daniel discovered this again when he, like his friends, determined to be obedient even unto death. After refusing to stop praying to his God, Daniel was thrown into a lions' den. A stone covered the tomb of this death trap. By that time, Daniel was almost eighty years old. The mere thought of staring into a lion's mouth could have given anyone his age a heart attack.

But another strange thing happened: Daniel walked out unscathed. Perhaps the lions were old, toothless, and arthritic. Maybe the den was abandoned.

But just so no one would misunderstand, Daniel recorded these words: "No wound was found on him, because he had trusted in his God." He further added, "The men who had falsely accused Daniel were brought in and thrown into the lions' den, along with their wives and children. And before they reached the floor of the den, the lions overpowered them and crushed all their bones" (Dan. 6:23–24). Hmmm.

Centuries later, people tried to explain away the miracle when a huge stone was rolled away from the tomb of a Man who chose obedience to God, even to his death. Rumors circulated because others didn't understand, and they couldn't explain the joy of the five-hundred-plus followers who saw Jesus once dead, now living (see 1 Corinthians 15:6).

The secret was no longer a secret. The God of heaven is also the God Who Lives Among Us. That good news is still bringing personal joy to anyone who has the faith to believe.

### PERSONAL TRUTH

*Our biggest test of faith and trust may lie in those three little words: "But if not . . ."*

### PERSONAL PRAYER

*Lord, what a joy to know that nothing, absolutely nothing, can defeat you. Give us the courage to stand for you no matter what the consequences. Thank you that even in the fire, you will always be with us.*

### PERSONAL QUESTION

*What has been your greatest test of faith?*

# THE GOD OF HIGH HILLS

*The LORD God is my strength;*
*He will make my feet like deer's feet,*
*And He will make me walk on my high hills.*

—Habakkuk 3:19 NKJV

The prophet Habakkuk found no reason for joy in his particular situation. All he could see in his own nation was injustice, pride, violence, and evil. Where was God in all this? Why did so many innocent people suffer, he wondered. Why didn't God prevent destruction, or at least end it?

It's a familiar cry. People have asked those same questions since God first made man. And we, no doubt, have wondered the same thing. Where was God when over six million Jews were slaughtered? Why didn't God prevent the tragic events of September 11, 2001, in America? Why doesn't he stop the abuse of thousands of children and adults in virtually every place in the world? Why does God allow evil to run rampant? Why doesn't he halt needless bloodshed? More often, the questions emerge when tragedy affects us personally.

God answered Habakkuk by heating up the fire even more. He was going to allow a more wicked nation, Babylon, to punish Judah for its rebellion against God. That only confused Habakkuk more. So again, he poured out his complaints and questions to God: "If you are holy and righteous and everlasting, why do you even tolerate their kind of wickedness? How can you use someone like—them? They're the worst offenders of all."

> God would not tolerate injustice forever.

Then Habakkuk decided to camp out to watch and wait for God's answer. He would take his security blanket of knowledge and his belief that God would answer and station himself on the highest place he knew. Then he braced for the worst. He would not miss God's response.

But maybe he didn't climb high enough. God answered Habakkuk, but not in the way the prophet might like. "Keep watching," God says, "and write down what you see. You may think my answers are slow, but keep waiting, and write it clearly so everyone can read it. You must accept these things by faith. There will come a time when the earth will be filled with the knowledge of the glory of the Lord. There will be a time when evil will receive its due reward. I am still in my holy temple. I am still in control. And I'm always on time" (see Hab. 2).

Although Habakkuk didn't like God's answer, he began to "get it." God would not tolerate injustice forever. He would deal with the Babylonians and any others who bullied people using violence and perversion as a license for self-gratification.

But Habakkuk didn't learn to live by faith just by waiting in his crow's nest, looking through an earthly telescope for a heavenly sign. He learned it by "coming up higher."

The apostle John learned the same lesson in solitary confinement, as a castaway on a desert island near Ephesus. In a vision, a door opened to heaven and invited John to "come up here, and I will show you what must take place" (Rev. 4:1).

Oswald Chambers understood as well:

*A higher state of mind and spiritual vision can only be achieved through the higher practice of personal character. If you live up to the highest and best that you know in the outer level of your life, God will continually say to you, "Friend, come up even higher." . . . when God elevates you by His grace into heavenly places, you find a vast plateau where you can move about with ease.*[27]

Habakkuk must have found that higher plateau. How do we know? He discovered it in a prayer of surrender. He rehearsed the faithful reputation and character of God as if suddenly seeing him from a fresh perspective, with lips quivering, heart pounding, and legs trembling.

Then Habakkuk made his spiritual "ascension" and declaration of faith. In terms we might understand, he said essentially, "Though we are hit with the world's worst famine, and all the farm crops fail and our animals die, though Wall Street collapses, and our economy hits the blackest depression it's ever known, and we lose everything, even in this, I will find my joy in the Lord. I choose to be joyful" (see Hab. 3:17–18).

> Regardless of what's happening around them, those who truly enjoy God have learned to "come up higher" with him.

How could Habakkuk make such a statement? Because "the LORD God is my strength; / He will make my feet like deer's feet, / And He will make me walk on my high hills." Now if you're a woman, I didn't say high heels. But it's about the same meaning. The hind, or deer, knew how to climb the heights, but God also equipped his feet with "shoes" especially made for walking and running the rugged terrain of those "high hills."

Perhaps Habakkuk is no longer just standing precariously in these high hills. In God's strength, he now *walks* there.

Regardless of what's happening around them, those who truly enjoy God have learned to "come up higher" with him. The view is always better at the top.

## PERSONAL TRUTH

*Victory can come on the mountains or in the valleys—as long as the Lord is there with us.*

## PERSONAL PRAYER

*Lord, you have given me faith shoes made for walking, but sometimes my legs falter and my knees buckle. Whenever I'm tempted to look down and be discouraged, help me to find my joy and strength in you so I, too, can walk on my high hills.*

## PERSONAL QUESTION

*Have you walked on any high hills lately?*

# THE GIFT THAT LASTS

*I bring you good news of great joy that will be for all the people.*
*Today in the town of David a Savior*
*has been born to you; he is Christ the Lord.*

—Luke 2:10–11

Every year for as long as I can remember, my family has kept a Christmas tradition of opening gifts one at a time. What started in my family of origin continued, though we moved the opening of gifts from Christmas Eve to the time of our own family's custom—Christmas morning. When our little ones still lived at home, their anticipation grew steadily until the first leap into our beds early on Christmas morning: "Isn't it time?" Even then, "Santa" left only a gift or two unwrapped for the children. The main ceremony would begin right after we downed a quick breakfast. No one ever seemed to mind the wait.

Even today, cradling warm cups in our hands, we savor both fresh coffee and fresh memories for three or four hours. We stretch the time as long as we can. Christmas has taken a whole year to arrive, and we want to enjoy every minute of it, for as long as we can. One by one, each person takes turns opening one gift as we pass and pause around the circle. While ripping and tearing are allowed, jumping out of turn is not. After each person opens a gift, everyone gushes in an en-thusiastic chorus of *oohs* and *aahs* along with generous thanks to the giver, usually accompanied by warm hugs and kisses. And without exception, we save the best—and the most treas-ured gifts—until last.

**More wonderful than the gift itself were the love and sacrifice behind it.**

"Which one should I open next?" we ask family members, waiting for someone to re-spond. We rarely kept our secrets from each other—only from the one to whom each of us gave his/her particular gift.

"Not that one!" someone invariably cries. "Save that one for last! Open another one!" And like little children, we giggle and gawk, all thoroughly enjoying our Christmas treasure hunt.

Larry and I married young, and we could afford only very simple wedding rings. My small, solitary diamond had been lost for ten years when Larry replaced it one year, surprising me at Christmas. My tastes were simple, and I had never al-lowed myself to dream about expensive things. Nevertheless, Larry put great thought into surprising me at Christmas. But that replacement stone was an extravagant gift for our small budget and had a special significance for the two of us—sym-bolizing a new start after some rocky times. That was about fifteen years ago. I didn't think any Christmas could top that.

But last year was extra special. After our usual three-hour unwrapping on Christmas morning, we were almost finished. Coached by my husband, girls, and sons-in-law to "Open, Open!" I saw that only one package remained. The video cam-era whirred, aimed in my direction. Every camera in the house was focused on me. It was a Kodak moment.

When I opened the box, I found the most beautiful dia-mond ring I had ever seen. Set with twenty-one tiny diamonds, in trios of seven each, it sparkled with brilliance. Although it was not a pricey ring by some standards, I knew Larry had probably spent ten or twelve times our agreed-upon amount for gifts to each other. This was an extremely generous gift, for which Larry had personally saved for years.

But the best part was the significance of the ring itself—an anniversary ring. It stood for the eternal significance of love and marriage: past, present, and future. And to me, each cluster of seven diamonds represented completeness—a perfect love, a perfect gift. More wonderful than the gift itself were the love and sacrifice behind it. Needless to say, I love and enjoy that man!

Over two thousand years ago, God wanted to give us a special gift—one that would last forever, one that would represent his love: past, present, and future. God had given the world many wonderful gifts through the years, including a beautiful plan of creation, family, friends, his laws to help guide, his love and protection. He also gave hints and promises through the years of a gift that would come, one worth waiting for, one waiting to be unwrapped until just the right time.

Prophets foretold it, crying silently, "Isn't it time?" Great men of faith died believing the gift would arrive even before it was given. God had saved up for this special present for a long, long, time. It cost him a great deal.

Then one night the time came. God wrapped up his very best gift in swaddling clothes and presented it to the world.

> God wrapped up his very best gift in swaddling clothes and presented it to the world.

Heaven's cameras stood ready to capture this extraordinary moment and most incredible gift. Born of a virgin, the gift was accompanied by a heavenly chorus of *oohs* and *aahs*, a spectacle witnessed by shepherds and angels alike. And just as the angels had announced earlier, the entire gift-giving celebration indeed brought great joy. This Gift, named Jesus, was none other than the Son of God, the Savior of the world.

It was God's very best personal Gift to you and to me, one that would truly last forever, bringing us his perfect love and joy—past, present, and future.

It's hard to believe some have never opened this exquisite Gift for themselves. Those who have already unwrapped theirs stand nearby, coaching and waiting with cameras in hand, crying, "Open! Open!" It's a Kodak moment.

Is it your turn to open his Gift?

## PERSONAL TRUTH

*Sometimes, the very best gifts are those that cost the most.*

## PERSONAL PRAYER

*Lord, thank you for giving your very best Gift to us—and for the joy that keeps on going and going and going.*

## PERSONAL QUESTION

*How has God's Christmas Gift blessed you?*

# THE GOD OF SECOND CHANCES

*Also on that day, the Master for the second time*
*will reach out to bring back what's left of his scattered people.*
*. . . In the end there'll be a highway all the way from Assyria,*
*easy traveling for what's left of God's people.*

—Isaiah 11:11, 16 MSG

On one hand, God exercised strong discipline on Judah and Israel. He purposefully used Assyria's enemy to bring judgment on Judah's rebellious, sinful ways. When two neighboring nations invaded Judah, the prophet Isaiah warned Ahaz the king of Judah to "keep calm" and not to "lose heart." But Ahaz would not listen. Instead of trusting God, he signed a treaty with a godless nation—the Assyrians. Whatever help Ahaz expected didn't materialize. And King Ahaz grew even more unfaithful to the Lord, closing the doors of the Lord's temple and building altars throughout Judah to worship other gods (see Isaiah 7:1-5, 12; 2 Chron. 28:16, 22-24).

Isaiah continued to warn his people, but their disobedience ushered in God's discipline. When the time came, Assyria had no clue God was using them to bring judgment on Judah, as well as nations like Israel. In time, he would destroy Assyria for their own prideful sin (see Isaiah 10:5-7, 12). Yet almost in the same breath, as he spoke through his servant Isaiah, God revealed that his tender heart had already planned a second chance for the remnant of his exiled people. It was a plan that began long before the foundation of the world. God is a God of Second Chances!

> God does not keep his anger forever; he is just and brings discipline always at the right moment.

God does not keep his anger forever; he is just and brings discipline always at the right moment. But those who came wandering out of exile—where would they go? Were they left to wander again on their own like a people without a country?

No, God has never left his people alone, and he never will. He has a covenant with them. Although the Israelites had locked themselves into an endless cycle of rebellion and rescue, God's mercy had no end.

Like an eerie picture from a sci-fi movie, we can almost imagine Isaiah's metaphor. The exiles approach what looks like the end of their journey, and as they trudge to the edge of the cliff, a "highway" appears to connect them from one mountain pass to another. That highway is none other than the promised Messiah himself.

History has proved these Scriptures. The prophet Micah recorded these words regarding Israel: "The day for building your walls will come, the day for extending your boundaries. In that day people will come to you from Assyria and the cities of Egypt. . . . Who is a God like you, who pardons sin and forgives the transgression of the remnant of his inheritance? (Micah 7:11-12, 18). Through the years of scourges and holocausts and terrorism, God's remnant still lives, gathered in a temporary place called "home" on earth. Only now the highway extends to Jews and Gentiles alike.

Isaiah even alludes to a future beyond already fulfilled prophecies. One day when Christ comes a second time, all nations will know—and see—a highway of eternal proportions. God's kingdom will restore all that was lost, and he will reclaim forever what his enemies tried to devour.

No matter how many times we turn aside from his highway, if we know God personally we, as exiles from lives lived much too long in bondage, can find our way back to this road. One step of faith places us on solid ground and back in his hands—once again in a position to enjoy this God of Second Chances.

Glenda knows about second chances. When a drunk driver killed her younger brother, Glenda's mom wanted to pursue a prison sentence for the young woman who had been driving. But after time and much prayer, Glenda began talking to her mother about rethinking her decision. "She's so young. Instead of exiling her to prison, let's ask the judge to give her a ten-year parole with intense community service. If she is involved with other families who have lost loved ones in similar circumstances, she will come to know the pain they feel. That kind of sentence will be much more effective than prison, and it will give her an opportunity to see how alcohol can destroy lives. Let's ask the judge to give her a second chance."

> God's love has already made provision for our self-induced detours into exile.

Her mom was reluctant, but God softened her heart and she finally agreed. The judge consented to the parole and community service, and the "exiled" woman enrolled in the program.

Glenda's mother told her later, "I am so glad you convinced me to give her a second chance. I could never have let go of this bitterness if I had not been willing to forgive."

John Greenleaf Whittier once wrote, "For of all sad words of tongue or pen, the saddest are these: 'It might have been!'" But because of God's grace and forgiveness, some things can still be. God's love has already made provision for our self-induced detours into exile. He never wants us to turn away from him. But should that happen, we can pray that the God of Second Chances will keep our hearts soft enough and our feet calloused enough to come back to his prepared highway.

There, the God who wants none to perish is always waiting to forgive with open arms.

### PERSONAL TRUTH

*God plans his celebration long before the prodigal returns home.*

### PERSONAL PRAYER

*Father, you have granted me so many second chances I have lost count. Like a magnet, your love draws me back again and again. You have forgiven me even though I don't deserve it. I owe you all my gratitude—because you do deserve it!*

### PERSONAL QUESTION

*What does being part of God's remnant mean to you?*

# THE GOOD SHEPHERD

*Suppose one of you has a hundred sheep and loses one of them.*
*Does he not leave the ninety-nine in the open country*
*and go after the lost sheep until he finds it?*

—Luke 15:4

It was a dark and stormy night. Wolves howled in perfect chorus with the wind. The young shepherd paused, listening for any signs of danger to his sheep. Quickening his pace, he stretched out his rod to correct a straggling sheep. Steadily he moved closer to home, leading his flock to safety for the night. The shepherd had led his flock through deep valleys, watered them beside cool streams, and now he had to bed them down in the sheepfold near his home to protect them from the cold.

He loved those sheep. He knew them all by name. No one else would take the responsibility if something happened to his sheep. He took seriously his assignment: to be a faithful shepherd to his flock.

The shepherd smiled a moment, deep in thought as his mind transported him to another time and place. How often he had used his staff to correct wayward sheep. All it took was one stubborn animal with a mind of its own. Like a child daydreaming, that sheep would gaze off into the horizon, see a

175

greener pasture or a new, unexplored path, and run off in that direction. If the shepherd's carefully aimed stone didn't frighten him back, other sheep would follow him—even if the path dropped right off a cliff.

> No one could be lost, not even one.

They were not the smartest animals. But he loved them even more for their dependency on him. They needed him. And he treasured each of them. Many times, while out with the sheep, the shepherd had lain awake all night and stretched his own body across the entrance of a temporary sheepfold, to make sure the sheep stayed secure. Golden, glaring pairs of eyes would stare at him from the dark, accompanied by the shrill howls from the sheep's enemies as they moved closer, hoping for an easy kill.

The last sheep brought up the rear and scrambled into the fold. The shepherd surveyed the flock and began to count, calling his sheep by name: "Speckled . . . Gray-Eared . . . Black . . . Fluffy-White." Wait a minute. He must have miscounted. This time, he numbered the sheep now resting for the night: ninety-seven, ninety-eight, ninety-nine. . . .

No, it couldn't be! Concern spread across the shepherd's brow as he spoke the truth he didn't want to believe: "One is lost! One sheep is lost!"

Securing the gate, he left the slumbering sheep and started out on his mission. "I must find him!" Friends down the way heard the commotion, but they did not understand his concern. Instead, they yelled, "The storm out there is growing worse. You have ninety-nine in the fold. Celebrate those ninety-nine you have! Forget about the one who is lost. He's probably already dead, anyway!"

But only a shepherd could truly know—and understand. These were *his* father's sheep. They belonged in *his* flock. And he alone must find that one. He would not rest until he found his missing sheep. No one could be lost, not even one.

Back through the howling winds he trudged, head bent, ears open for the familiar bleating of his missing sheep. He knew exactly which one was gone: Brown, the headstrong lamb, had separated from its mother. It wasn't the first time the shepherd had rescued that lamb from danger. But never had it strayed this far, for this long. On he trekked, listening, calling out the sheep's name. He knew he was the only one who could rescue Brown. Sheep will run from a stranger, but Brown knew its shepherd's voice.

Up steep mountain passes he walked, remembering how he had escorted his sheep over the pass earlier that day. And then he heard it: the faint bleating of Brown's voice. The shepherd could see no sheep on the narrow mountain road. But the farther he climbed, the louder the bleating. As he rounded a sharp turn, he paused, peering over the edge of the road.

His eyes focusing on the direction of the sound, the shepherd paused to give thanks as the clouds parted and a faint glow of moonlight hovered over a brush-tree limb jutting out from beneath an overhanging rock. There he saw the little lamb, its wool matted and torn, tangled in the branches of the tree. Gently, carefully, the shepherd lay down, extending his rod to the neck of the lamb. Bracing one hand on the large rock for support, he inched his arm toward the lamb's body.

> As long as one is still lost, he will go to the ends of the earth to say, "I love you!"

Within minutes he held the lamb close to his chest. The shepherd poured oil on the badly bruised and bleeding sheep's wounds, then wrapped him securely around his strong shoulders. As they both neared home, others ran to greet the shepherd. "He found Brown! Brown is safe!" And as if on cue, the little lamb uttered a weak but grateful "Baaaaah!"

The story is only a parable. But Jesus told it with great passion. After all, it was a picture of his own Father's love for people. And it was a character profile of Jesus himself, the Good Shepherd. The Good Shepherd truly enjoys his sheep.

Jesus told his disciples, "I know my sheep, and they know my voice" (see John 10:14, 16). Not only that, Jesus is the gate itself on the sheepfold. In fact, he lay down his own life in death and was resurrected to life just to protect and to save his sheep from certain death.

Our heavenly Father is not content that ninety-nine remain safe in the sheepfold of his love and care. As long as one is still lost, he will go to the ends of the earth to say, "I love you!" Jesus says this of us, his "sheep": "I give them eternal life. No one can snatch them out of my Father's hand" (see John 10:28).

The shepherd and all his friends threw a party because they were so happy to see the lost sheep returned. And what of the sheep? Because the Bible calls us all "sheep," we have a clue as to how they felt (Isa. 53:6). Did you ever wonder why the psalmist felt God's rod and staff "comforted" him (Ps. 23:4)? If you've ever been lost for days, months, years, or even hours, how do you feel when someone finally finds you? I guarantee that among all your emotions, gratitude and joy will be right there at the top.

It may be a long time ago that you were "lost," and the Father found you wandering away from his sheepfold, or maybe even clinging to a tree limb. But some things you never forget. Those of us who have been there and done that have the scars to prove it.

Yes, we know well the feeling of joy.

## PERSONAL TRUTH

*Once you are his sheep, you are always his sheep.*

## PERSONAL PRAYER

*Lord, how comforting and tender you are with your lambs. Thank you for loving me enough to lay down your life so I could enjoy your eternal sheepfold.*

## PERSONAL QUESTION

*How has the Good Shepherd comforted you?*

# THE GOD WE APPLAUD

*On your feet now—applaud GOD!*
*. . . Enter with the password: "Thank you!"*
*. . . Thank him. Worship him.*

—Psalm 100:1, 4 MSG

Like many other churches, ours bought out the local theatre's tickets for several nights' showings of Mel Gibson's *The Passion of the Christ*. I looked forward to the night I would attend.

During the movie the crowd members watched intensely, often gripping the arms of their seats or grabbing tissues to dab away their tears. Scene after scene affected me personally as I viewed the suffering of Christ reenacted so vividly. When the last scene ended, everyone froze. It was as if every emotion had been drained from our bodies, and we felt paralyzed.

The screen had momentarily pictured Jesus' ascension, and for a split second something in me wanted to stand in victory. But I sat motionless, too moved to speak, while warm tears of gratitude trickled down my face. Just as the credits began to appear, we heard some commotion from the center of the theatre. A loud Texas whoop broke the icy silence, followed by a man's loud clapping. Although we all looked to see the source of the intrusion, no one else joined in his private celebration.

Only God knows, but I have a feeling no one thought the man's jubilation out of place. It was his personal way of expressing the ultimate joy of Jesus' death and resurrection.

In another intense setting one day, a man named David also let out a joyful whoop—only that time, someone objected strongly. That someone was none other than David's wife, Michal. David was leading a processional, bringing the ark of the covenant back to Jerusalem. The ark represented the presence of the Lord, and it had been neglected during King Saul's reign.

> The truth is the way each of us may choose to rejoice in the Lord will be different because we are not cookie-cutter Christians.

The Bible says David "danced with great abandon before GOD." But when David's wife saw him leaping and dancing before God, she was filled with disgust—and told him so: "How wonderfully the king has distinguished himself today—exposing himself to the eyes of the servants' maids like some burlesque street dancer!" (2 Sam. 6:14, 20 MSG).

David's paraphrased response sounded something like this: "I will gladly be a fool for the God I love, and I will dance for his glory far more recklessly than I've done here today. God's presence has been restored! That's something to be joyful about!" (see 2 Sam. 6:21–22).

The truth is the way each of us may choose to rejoice in the Lord will be different because we are not cookie-cutter Christians. God created each of us to be unique, and then he discarded the blueprints.

The angel's joyful announcement to Mary that she would bear the Son of God left her stunned at first, but then she responded gently, "I am the Lord's servant. May it be to me as you have said." A few months later, when Mary visited her pregnant cousin Elizabeth, the baby leaped in Elizabeth's womb at Jesus' presence inside Mary. Filled with God's Spirit, both women broke out in singing. Listen to some of Mary's words, which were later called the Magnificat: "My soul glorifies the Lord. . . . I'm dancing the song of my Savior God. . . . The Mighty One has done great things for me— / holy is his name" (Luke 1:46, 47 MSG, 49).

After Jesus was born, surrounded by a chorus of joyful angels, shepherds, and noisy animals, Mary remained silent. Perhaps her joy was too deep to vocalize. The Bible says, "Mary kept all these things to herself, holding them dear, deep within herself." The shepherds, on the other hand, "returned and let loose, glorifying and praising God for everything they had heard and seen" (Luke 2:19–20 MSG).

Scripture records myriad other joyful responses toward God: dancing, singing, clapping, laughing, playing instruments, shouting, kneeling, weeping, or lifting hands. One thing is certain: a true experience with God always brings a response—even if it is one of silent awe.

God doesn't want our expressions of joy to be influenced by taboos or fears, or what others think, but by the stirrings of God's Spirit within. He wants our hearts to leap with joy at the mention of his name. He desires the soaring of our spirits when we enter his presence. And he loves to see our reverence for him. He deserves our applause!

**He deserves our applause!**

Like Job, ponder the greatness of God. Join David as he meditated on God's grace and goodness. Place your shoes beside Moses' and walk upon holy ground. Let your tears of gratitude mingle with Mary's as she bathed the feet of Jesus. Cry out with Isaiah in realization of your nothingness and God's sovereignty.

Rejoice with Peter, John, Mary, Martha, Thomas, and the martyrs who loved him until their deaths. Shout with them, "He is risen! He is alive!"

Some days I find myself feeling like David, hands raised and dancing with great abandon before God. Other times I fall on my face, weeping at his great sacrifice for me. And some mornings I race to my journal, pouring out the contents of a grateful heart, using my pen as the microphone of my soul. Some days the joy wells up so strong that, like Jeremiah, I cannot contain it. I feel "overpowered" and long to share with someone the reason for my joy.

How we express our joy is not as important as that we do express it. He knows our hearts. And after all, it's really not for us. It's for the God We Applaud.

### PERSONAL TRUTH

*Our emotions may change, but God never does.*

### PERSONAL PRAYER

*Lord, how can I ever express my joy to you adequately? No words, no emotion, no language on earth would ever be enough. God, I applaud you with my whole heart!*

### PERSONAL QUESTION

*How do you like to applaud God best?*

# AUTHOR'S NOTE

Perhaps you have never come to know and enjoy the intimate presence of God personally. If He has placed such a desire in your heart, may I share with you some simple steps so you can become acquainted with Him and become a child of God forever?

1. Admit the sin in your life and the need in your heart for God (see Rom. 3:23).

2. Acknowledge that Jesus loves you and that he died for your sin (see John 3:16).

3. Recognize his salvation is a gift, and not something earned (see Eph. 2:8-9, Rom. 6:23).

4. Ask Jesus to forgive you, to come into your life, and to fill you with his personal, intimate presence (see Rev. 3:20).

5. By faith, thank him that you are now God's child, and confess that from now on, he will be the Lord and Love of your life. Give Jesus the key to all the rooms of your heart (see Rom. 10:9-10, John 1:12).

I hope this book has encouraged you. If I can help your Christian growth in any way, please let me know. You can drop me a line at my Web site at www.rebeccabarlowjordan.com.

*Rebecca Barlow Jordan*

# NOTES

1. Richard J. Foster, *Prayer: Finding the Heart's True Home* (San Francisco: HarperSanFrancisco, 1992), 142.

2. Oswald Chambers, *My Utmost for His Highest* (Grand Rapids, MI: Discovery House Publishers, 1992), February 19.

3. Brother Lawrence and Teresa of Avila, *The Practice of the Presence of God, The Way of Perfection* (Nashville, TN: Thomas Nelson, Inc. 1999), 12.

4. Henry Drummond, *The Greatest Thing in the World* (London and Glasgow: Collins, 1962), 52, 55–56.

5. Chambers, *My Utmost*, March 19.

6. Bruce Larson as quoted by Charles R. Swindoll in *The Tale of the Tardy Oxcart* (Nashville, TN: Word Publishing, 1998), 609.

7. E. C. McKenzie, *14,000 Quips and Quotes* (Grand Rapids, MI: Baker Books, 1980), 420.

8. Chambers, *My Utmost*, June 3.

9. J. I. Packer, *Knowing God* (Downers Grove, IL: Intervarsity Press, 1973), 39–40

10. Packer, 39.

11. Leslie B. Flynn, *Come Alive with Illustrations* (Grand Rapids, MI: Baker Books, 1988), 180.

12. Steve Kenny, "Couple Fell in Love 'Somewhere Along the Way,'" *Dallas Morning News*, March 27, 2005, 9E.

13. Amelia Feathers, "Mother Overcomes Handicap to Live a Full and Happy Life," *Orange Leader*, reprinted in *Greenville Herald Banner*, January 19, 1998, A-5.

14. Hannah Whitall Smith, *The Christian's Secret of a Happy Life* (Old Tappan, NJ: Fleming H. Revell Company, 1942), 107.

15. Martin Luther from *The Encyclopedia of Religious Quotations*, edited by Frank S. Mead (Westwood, NJ: Fleming H. Revell Company, 1965), 227.

16. Iris and Duane Blue as told to Jon Kent Walker, "From Checkered Past to Amazing Grace," *Home Life*, July 1999, 14–18.

17. The Internet Fraud Complaint Center (IFCC) 2002 Internet Fraud Report, January 1, 2002–December 31, 2002, prepared by the National White Collar Crime Center and the Federal Bureau of Investigation, http://www.ifccfbi.gov/strategy/2002_IFCC Report.pdf.

18. "Top 10 Work At Home and Home Based Business Scams," Issue #61, Audri and Jim Lanford, http://www.scambusters.org/work-at-home.html, April 23, 2003.

19. "Nigerian Scam," Issue #11, Audri and Jim Lanford, http://www.scambusters.org/NigerianFee.html, April 23, 2003.

20. The Internet Fraud Complaint Center (IFCC) 2002 Internet Fraud Report.

21. "Nigerian Scams: Why Do People Fall for Them?" Issue #83, Audri and Jim Lanford, http://www.scambusters.org/nigerian-scams.html, July 7, 2004.

22. Janet Wilson, "Who Heals the Healer?" *Baptist Standard*, April 10, 2000.

23. Mildred Tengbom, *Grief for a Season* (Minneapolis, MN: Bethany House Publishers, 1989), 136.

24. Foster, *Prayer*, 134.

25. Rick Warren, *The Purpose Driven Life* (Grand Rapids, MI: Zondervan, 2002), 63.

26. Anna Quindlen, *A Short Guide to a Happy Life* (New York: Random House, 2000), 10, 15, 20, 45–46.

27. Chambers, *My Utmost*, March 27.

Also from Rebecca Barlow Jordan

# 40 Days in God's Blessing

Do believers really understand what it means to live in God's blessing? To truly experience his grace? Unfortunately, many people would have to answer no. Many don't understand *how* to believe in God's blessing. They don't know how to open their hands, their eyes, their hearts to his affection.

In *40 Days in God's Blessing*, Rebecca Barlow Jordan invites readers to walk in the shadow of those gone before—to trace the footprints of God's faithfulness through the lives of other believers who were blessed. Through these character studies, readers are brought face to face with the God who loves them more than they can imagine. They are encouraged to seek out the God who wants to gift them with immeasurable grace.

God's blessings are found in the most unexpected moments. By spending just forty days with God, readers will come to realize the blessings waiting especially for them.

*Available July 2006*